Gingerbread Kids

Super Easy Activities to Help Young Children Learn

Created and written by
Jenett Patrick

Text illustrated by
Sara Mittelstaedt

Published by Pp PARTNER PRESS
Box 124
Livonia, MI 48152

ISBN 0-933212-40-2

Distributed by:

Gryphon House
3706 Otis Street
Mt. Rainier, Maryland 20822

ACKNOWLEDGEMENTS

I would like to express my gratitude to my three grown children, Jennifer, Tim, and Sheila, who inspired me to create and develop the original dolls twenty years ago. I want to especially thank my husband, Duane, who encouraged and supported my endeavor. A special word of thanks goes to my friend, Margaret Breckon, who spent many hours reading, discussing, and aiding in the improvement of my drafts. My appreciation to Sheryl Brogger and Nancy Hicok, my patient typists. I would also like to thank Joyce King for her excellent professional assistance in editing. And special acknowledgement to my son, Tim, for his cover idea.

Jenett Patrick

FOREWORD

Jenette Patrick firmly believes that tremendous and rewarding advantages can be gained through the use of the paper dolls incorporated in this book. Not only can it be a major management technique, but it is an excellent teaching aid. Gingerbread Kids is the result of 25 years of teaching, collecting, learning, and having three children of her own. The author hopes you have as good a time using the book as she has had during the years of developing these techniques.

 **<u>PREFACE</u>**

As we become more aware of each child's developmental age, it is significant for us to provide additional creative materials. This book and its activities seek to do so. The rationale and readings of Piaget, Montessori, Getman, Gessell, and Kephart have influenced my desire to provide this book and activities for all young children. I have also been influenced by the needs of my own children and the children in my classroom.

The purpose of this book is to offer activities for the child in Pre-Kindergarten, Kindergarten, Pre-First Grade, First Grade (grade placement or developmentally), and the special needs child in a happy, fun, creative, and positive way. The book covers community helpers, body awareness, eight basic colors, role-playing, cutting and manipulation skills, sensorimotor skills and creativity. The units also include other activities. They are: fingerplays, field trips, art projects, experience stories, and personal journals. The units can be completed in two to five days in 15 to 25 minute time blocks.

The paper dolls and activities found in this book are utilized to introduce and develop the following concepts:

1. The paper dolls and activities provide happy, healthy, and positive experiences that develop strong self-concept, self-worth, self-respect, respect for others, and the courage to take risks.

2. The paper dolls and activities provide the opportunity to learn how to classify, organize, sequence, sort, match likenesses and differences, and attend to task.

3. The paper dolls and activities provide individualization for the child at his/her level of development in a flexible and consistent atmosphere with emphasis on the total child.

4. The paper dolls and activities provide sensorimotor skill training and experience essential to the child's understanding and adjustment to the world, persons, things, ideas, and self.

5. The paper dolls and activities provide opportunities for active manipulation and exploration of materials in order to understand how certain phenomena take place while stimulating and expanding his/her creativity and imagination.

6. The paper dolls and activities provide the child time to visualize, share his/her ideas and thoughts, and to develop his/her knowledge.

7. The paper dolls and activities provide for the psycholinguistic needs of the child as follows:

    a. auditory and visual reception
    b. auditory and visual association
    c. verbal expression
    d. visual and auditory closure
    e. auditory and visual sequential memory
    f. manual and motor needs

8. The paper dolls and associated suggestions provide spontaneous activities for children's free time.

9. The paper dolls and activities assist the teacher in gaining insight and understanding of each individual.

TABLE OF CONTENTS

Acknowledgements iii
Foreword iv
Preface v

PART 1 - UNITS

Organization for First Day 1
THE GINGERBREAD BOY 3
Unit 1 - Meeting Doll 6
Unit 2 - School Bus 10
Unit 3 - Sleepy Time 14
Unit 4 - Breakfast 18
Unit 5 - Party Day 22
Unit 6 - Swimming 25
Unit 7 - Dentist and Teeth 31
Unit 8 - Fire Fighter and Fire Station 35
Unit 9 - Library 39
Unit 10 - Bakery 43
Unit 11 - Apple Orchard 47
Unit 12 - Hair Care 51
Unit 13 - Doctor and Nurse 55
Unit 14 - Police Officers 59
Unit 15 - Dairy Farm, Milk and Butter 63
Unit 16 - Stone Soup and Grocery Store 68
Unit 17 - Our House and Family 72
Unit 18 - Halloween 77
Unit 19 - Balloons 82
Unit 20 - Math Activities 86
Unit 21 - Color and The Gingerbread Boy 88

PART 11 - PATTERNS

Girl Doll 89
Boy Doll 90
Basic Clothing Pattern Number 1 . . . . 91, 92
Basic Clothing Pattern Number 2 93
Unit 2 Coat and Hat 95
Unit 3 Night Clothes 96, 97
Unit 4 School Clothing 98, 99
Unit 5 Party Clothing 100, 101
Unit 6 Swim Suits 102
Unit 7 Outfit To Go To Dentist 103, 104
Unit 8 Fire Fighter Clothing 105, 106
Unit 9 Jeans Clothing 107
Unit 10 Baker Clothing 108, 109, 110
Unit 13 Doctor and Nurse Clothing 111, 112, 113, 115
Unit 14 Police Officer Clothing 106, 114
Unit 15 Farmer Clothing 115, 116
House Journal Pattern 117
Apple Journal Pattern 118
Index 119

ORGANIZATION FOR FIRST DAY

Materials

Scissors
Paint
Doll master pattern
12" x 18" white or light brown lightweight tagboard
Laminating machine
10" x 14" envelopes

Procedure

1. Reproduce the dolls (pages 89 and 90) on a lightweight tagboard by tracing around the master pattern. Make one doll for each boy and girl in the class (boy can be called "Molasses" and girl can be called "Ginger"). Make two more of each; extras may be needed.

2. Paint and decorate. Write each child's name on the back of his/her doll.* Decorate as per the examples of the master pattern. Use felt tip pens or tempera paint to color red on the back of the right hand and green on the left hand when face down.

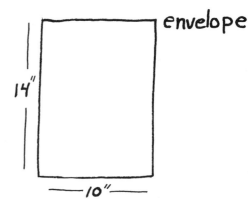

3. Have the dolls laminated. If laminating materials are not available, cover the dolls with clear contact paper.

4. Place the dolls in 10" x 14" envelopes with the child's name on the outside and place on each child's desk/table for the first day of school.*

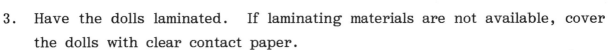

*Labeling the dolls and envelopes helps children keep track of their own dolls and clothes. It also helps them find and recognize their own names and other children's names. The envelope is excellent for storage. The children can store

1

their dolls and clothes in their envelopes for the duration of the activities to follow. The envelopes can be kept in their desks or stacked together on a table and taken out when desired. At the end of each activity, have the children place the clothes and dolls back in their envelopes for the next time. This is training for organization and care of materials.

THE GINGERBREAD BOY

Once upon a time, there was a little old woman and a little old man who lived in a pretty little white house near a winding road. The little old woman and the little old man were very happy, but they wanted a little boy.

So, one day when the little old woman was baking cookies, she said, "I will make a little gingerbread boy."

He had two raisins for eyes, a red jelly bean for a nose, and shiny red frosting for a mouth. The little old woman gave him black licorice hair, raisins for buttons, and frosting for shoes and trim. He was very handsome, indeed.

She placed him carefully in the oven to bake. When the little old woman looked in the oven, the gingerbread boy was puffy and brown. The gingerbread boy jumped out of the oven and ran out of the house.

The little woman screamed, "Stop, stop!" But the gingerbread boy kept running and ran past the little old man who was pulling weeds out of the green beans, yellow corn, and orange carrots.

"Stop, stop!" the little old man cried. But the gingerbread boy only ran on and said, "Run, run as fast as you can. You can't catch me, I'm the gingerbread boy."

The gingerbread boy ran on until he came to a red cow in a big green field.

"Stop, stop!" said the red cow. The gingerbread boy laughed and said, "Run, run as fast as you can. You can't catch me, I'm the gingerbread boy. I ran away from a little old woman and a little old man, and I can run away from you, I can, I can." And the red cow couldn't catch him either.

Off he ran down the road where he saw a black horse in a grown field.

"Stop, stop!" said the black horse. The gingerbread boy laughed and said, "Run, run as fast as you can. You can't catch me, I'm the gingerbread boy. I ran away from the little old woman and the little old man and the red cow, and I can run away from you, I can, I can." And away he ran, and the black horse couldn't catch him either.

Off he ran to the green woods where a fat brown rabbit lived.

"Stop, stop!" called the fat brown rabbit. But the gingerbread boy called back, "Run, run as fast as you can. You can't catch me, I'm the gingerbread boy. I ran away from the little old woman and the little old man and the red cow and the black horse, and I can run away from you, I can, I can." And away he ran, and the fat brown rabbit couldn't catch him either.

Then, the gingerbread boy was sure nobody could catch him.

Just then a big orange fox called out, "Stop, stop!" And the gingerbread boy said, "Run, run as fast as you can. You can't catch me, I'm the gingerbread boy. I ran away from the little old woman and the little old man and the red cow and the black horse and the fat brown rabbit, and I can run away from you, I can, I can." And he ran and ran until he came to a wide blue river and stopped by the purple flowers.

The big orange fox ran up beside him and answered, "Catch you? I only wanted to run with you and help you cross the wide blue river. Get on my tail."

So the gingerbread boy got on the tail of the big orange fox, and the big orange fox started across the wide blue river.

Soon the big orange fox said, "Jump on my back and you'll be dry." So the gingerbread boy jumped on the back of the big orange fox.

The water became deeper and the yellow sun shone brighter and the big orange fox said, "Get up on my nose so you don't get wet." And so the gingerbread boy jumped up on the nose of the big orange fox.

The gingerbread boy never did get to the other side of the river. But the big orange fox was very, very happy as he climbed out of the wide blue river.

UNIT 1 - MEETING DOLL

It is best to do this unit within one to three days after school starts in the fall.

Goal

To initiate introductions and present the Gingerbread Doll to the children.

Objectives

1. To provide experience in introduction skills.
2. To provide practice using full name.
3. To provide exploration and development of coloring, cutting, manipulation and creating.
4. To provide visual awareness of self and others.
5. To provide activities to develop body and space awareness.

Materials

Doll and 10" x 14" envelope for each child
Scissors
Crayons
9" x 12" white construction paper
Unit 1 Basic Clothing Patterns

Procedure

1. Read or tell <u>The Gingerbread Boy</u> story to the children.

2. Reproduce Unit 1 Boy/Girl Basic Clothing Pattern Number 1 (pages 91 and 92) on white construction paper. Make at least two or three more patterns than the number of children.

3. Give each child his/her doll and introduce the doll to the child.

4. Have each child introduce himself/herself to his/her doll. "My name is _____(Full name)_____." Pattern this exercise with the children before they introduce themselves to the doll, saying twice with you and twice by themselves.

5. Give each child his/her clothing.

6. Have each child tell a partner what he/she is wearing to school that day. Have the children design the clothing like the clothes they have on.

7. Have each child cut out the clothes he/she designed. A heavy cutting line helps the child with figure ground and helps him/her avoid cutting off the tabs. Some developmental kindergarteners will need them cut out the first few times or use double-holed scissors with the aid of the teacher. The amount of teacher help and individualization needed will depend on the <u>developmental age</u> of the child. Have each child put his/her name on the back of his/her clothes to eliminate confusion of whose is whose when playing together. If the child is unable to write his/her own name, do it for him/her or give assistance.

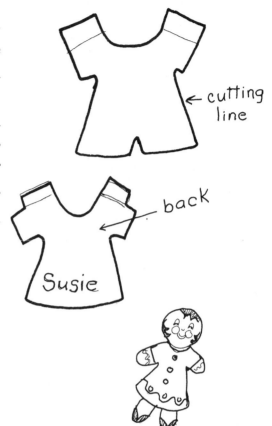

8. Have them put the clothes on the doll.

9. Have the children introduce their dolls to the persons behind/beside them. Make sure everyone has a partner. Let them have two or three minutes to visit.

10. Have each child return the doll and clothing to his/her envelope for storage after all the activities.

Enrichment Activities

1. Let the children play with their dolls during free time.

2. Have the children bring pictures of themselves to post on the bulletin board.

3. Have the children draw pictures of themselves to post on the bulletin board.

4. Have them look in a full-length mirror and introduce themselves and their dolls.

5. Write a total class experience story about each child's family.

   Example: Jimmy has a mom, a dad, one sister, and a cat.

         Susie has a dad, two sisters, and a grandma.

   Let each child tell his/her story. Write the experience story on chart paper so all the children can see their stories.

   Families

   Jimmy has:

6. Fingerplays:

   A. <u>THIS IS ME</u>

   Here are my ears, (Touch ears)

   Here is my nose, (Touch nose)

   Here are my fingers, (Touch fingers)

   And here are my toes. (Touch toes)

   Here are my eyes, (Touch eyes)

   Opened so wide, (Open eyes wide)

   Here is my mouth with my teeth inside.

       (Touch mouth, point to teeth)

   Here is my tongue to help me speak. (Point to tongue)

   Here is my chin (Touch chin)

   And here are my cheeks. (Touch cheeks)

   Here are my hands that help me play, (Show hands)

   And here are my feet that run all day. (Show feet)

   B. <u>ONE LITTLE CHILD</u>

   Two little feet go tap, tap, tap. (Tap feet three times)

   Two little hands go clap, clap, clap. (Clap hands three times)

   A quick little leap up from the chair. (Leap from chair)

   Two little arms reach high in the air. (Reach high)

   Two little feet go jump, jump, jump. (Jump three times)

   Two little hands go thump, thump, thump. (Thump hands three times)

   One little body turns around and around. (Turn three times)

   One little child sits quietly down. (Sit down)

   But the brownie who is tiny, if he'd try, try, try,

       (Get as small as possible)

   Might reach up to the giant who is high, high, high.

       (Stand and reach tall)

C. <u>IMAGINE</u>

    <u>   (Child's name)   </u>   stand up. (Child stands up)

Can you imagine a giant who is tall, tall, tall? (Reach and stand tall)

Can you imagine a brownie who is small, small, small? (Bend or sit)

9

UNIT 2 - SCHOOL BUS

Goal

To develop bus-riding skills.

Objectives

1. To provide exploration and development of coloring, cutting, manipulating, and creating.
2. To provide experience in verbal expression.
3. To provide activities to develop body and space awareness.
4. To provide awareness of safety on, off, and around the bus.
5. To provide the child with confidence and knowledge of location of his/her school bus.
6. To provide an awareness of the color yellow.

Materials

Doll
Scissors
Crayons
9" x 12" white construction paper
12" x 18" white construction paper
12" x 18" yellow construction paper
Newsprint
Unit 2 Clothing Patterns
House Journal Pattern

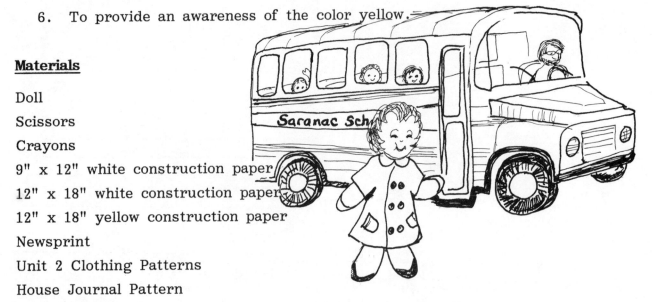

Procedure

1. Reproduce Unit 2 Boy/Girl Coat and Hat (pages 94 and 95) on white paper. Make a few extras.

2. Explain the need for wearing coats and hats to school. Give each child his/her coat and hat patterns.

3. Have each child color the clothing the way he/she wishes and add desired designs.

4. Have the child cut the clothing on the heavy line and try it on the paper doll, following their developmental age (Unit 1, Procedure 7).

10

5. Have the children put their names on the back of their clothing to eliminate confusion. Encourage them to copy their names from the back of the doll or envelope.

6. Discuss school bus safety:
   a. Remain in your seat.
   b. Sit quietly on the bus.
   c. Leave and enter in a single file.
   d. Be considerate of others on the bus.
   e. Discuss finding the correct bus.

7. Role-play sitting on a school bus. Have the children sit in rows as if they are on a school bus. Have them hold their dolls while role-playing.

8. Have the children return the dolls and clothing to their envelopes for storage after all activities.

Enrichment Activities

1. Have the children make a bus from 12" x 18" yellow construction paper. Make a label with the school name on it for the side of the bus. Have the children draw pictures of themselves on the bus. Cut the bus out. Role-play bus safety with the doll using the paper school bus. Introduce the color yellow, via the bus.

2. Using the House Journal Pattern (page 117), make a booklet shaped like a house for each child. Use a folded 12" x 18" sheet of white construction paper for the cover. Use newsprint for the 15 pages. Staple at the fold. Have the children design their own covers and write their names on them.

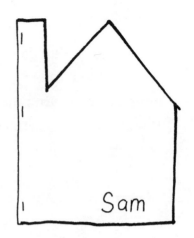

The journal helps the children learn to turn pages from the front to the back, and read from left to right. It is also advantageous for language and reading development. It is suggested that the teacher write the following journal stories in the first pages: "My Family," "My House," "My Pet," and "Me." First the children draw a picture on the page. Then they tell the teacher about it. Finally, the teacher may record the story in the child's journal.

3. Discuss sitting down on the bus. Also, explain that it is important to cross at least 20 feet in front of the bus so the driver can see them cross the road. Practice in a bus parking area so the children are aware of the distance. Also, practice looking from left to right as they cross in front of the bus.

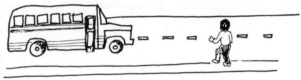

4. Have the children write a class experience story about riding on a bus.

5. Fingerplay:

   A. ON THE BUS
   The wheels on the bus go round and round.
       (Make hands go around)
   The students on the bus go up and down.
       (Children go up and down in their chairs)
   The windshield wipers go back and forth.
       (Children make hands go left and right)
   The bus driver goes rrr, rrr, rrr, down the road.
       (Pretend to drive bus)

6. Ask the children how they move their head, hands, eyes, feet, legs, knees, ankles, toes, fingers, mouth, eyes, waist, hips, wrists, arms, chest, and neck. Have them show how they do it.

7. Game: "Gingerbread Doll Says"

    Have the children respond to the following:

    Gingerbread Doll says touch your neck,
        "   "   "   touch your head,
        "   "   "   touch your nose,
        "   "   "   blink your eyes,
        "   "   "   wave your hands,
        "   "   "   bend your stomach,
        "   "   "   lift your leg,
        "   "   "   touch your ears,
        "   "   "   open your mouth.

8. Have each child draw a picture in his/her journal about riding a bus. Then have the child tell the teacher a story about the bus ride. Record the story in the child's journal with or without the teacher's assistance.

UNIT 3 - SLEEPY TIME

Goal

To develop an understanding of the need for sleep.

Objectives

1. To provide exploration and development of coloring, cutting, manipulating, and creating.
2. To provide experiences to develop body and space awareness.
3. To provide verbal expression experience.
4. To provide awareness of the importance of sleep.

Materials

Scissors
Crayons
9" x 12" white construction paper
Doll
Shoe boxes (one for each child)
4" x 9" colored construction paper
Large pieces of paper (size of child)
Scraps of construction paper
Paste
Unit 3 Clothing Patterns
House Journal

Procedure

1. Reproduce Unit 3 Boy/Girl Night Clothes (pages 96 and 97) on white paper. Make a few extras.

2. Give each child his/her clothing.

3. Have each child color and add desired designs to his/her P.J.'s and nighties.

4. Have the child cut out the clothing on the heavy line, remembering his/her developmental age (Unit 1, Procedure 7). Have the child try the clothing on the doll.

5. Have the children put their names on the back of their clothing to eliminate confusion. (Some children may need assistance with this task.) Encourage them to copy their names from the back of the doll or envelope.

6. Make beds out of shoe boxes. Color the sheets and the pillows. Give each child a piece of 4" x 9" colored construction paper to color and design a blanket for the bed. Put the doll in the bed. Label each box with the child's name.

7. Discuss going to bed and the need for sleep. Make a list of reasons why we need our sleep. Let the children give you their ideas. Help them find the most important reason, such as: it helps us grow, builds strong minds and bodies, or helps us to be calm and happy.

8. Stack "box-beds" in storage area for use again. Have each child return the doll and clothing to his/her envelope for storage after all activities.

Enrichment Activities

1. Let the children pretend they are parents while putting their dolls to bed.

2. Give them free time to share and play with each other and their dolls.

3. Have the children draw pictures in their personal journals of themselves sleeping in bed. Have them tell stories about "Why We Sleep." Record the stories in their journals.

4. Suggested reading:
   Sleep. John Mousedale. New York: Wonder Books, 1972.
   Sleep Is For Everyone. Paul Showers. New York: Thomas Y. Crowell Company, 1974.

5. Fingerplays:

A. <u>GOING TO BED</u>
This little boy is just going to bed,
 (Lay forefinger in palm of hand)
Down on the pillow he lays his head;
 (Thumb acts as pillow)
Wraps himself in his blankets tight,
 (Wrap fingers around "boy")
And this is the way he sleeps all night.
 (Close eyes)
Morning comes and he opens his eyes,
 (Open eyes)
Back with a toss, the cover flies;
 (Open fingers)
Soon he is up and dressed and away,
 (Forefinger stands straight)
Ready for school and ready for play.

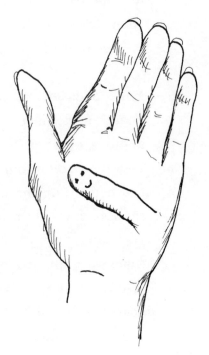

B. <u>GRANDMA'S</u>
These are Grandma's spectacles
 (Make glasses with thumb and forefinger)
This is Grandma's hat;
 (Fingers form a peak on top of head)
This is the way she folds her hands and lays them in her lap.
 (Fold hands and place in lap)
These are Grandma's knives and forks
 (Hold up hand, pretending to hold fork and knife)
This is mother's table;
 (Hands form a table, fingers top, thumbs legs)
This is sister's looking glass
 (Thumbs touching forefinger, form circle)
And this is baby's cradle.
 (Fingers laced easily, rock hands and arms back and forth)

C. **NIGHT TIME**

Before I jump into my bed (Child jumps)

Before I dim my light (Pretend to turn off light)

I put my shoes together (Put hands together)

So they can talk at night.

I'm sure they would be lonesome

If I tossed one here and there, (Toss hands)

So I put them close together (Hands back together)

For they're a friendly pair.

6. Have the children touch parts of their bodies as demonstrated by the teacher.

Touch head	Touch arms
" ears	" hands
" nose	" elbows
" mouth	" chest
" eyes	" stomach
" neck	" shoulders
" legs	" ankles
" knees	" toes
" waist	" fingers
" wrists	" cheeks

Then have them touch these body parts on their paper dolls as said and touched by the teacher.

7. Place large pieces of paper on the floor, one for each child. With partners, have each child draw around the other. Have the child color his/her outline and cut it out. (This may take two sessions.) After the child has cut out the outline, put his/her name on it with a magic marker. Encourage them to add buttons, pockets, eyes, noses, eyebrows, ears, hair, and mouth. Hands and feet can also be made of colored paper and pasted to the self-portrait.

17

UNIT 4 - BREAKFAST

Goal

To develop an awareness of the need for a good breakfast.

Objectives

1. To provide exploration and development of coloring, cutting, manipulating, and creating.
2. To provide experience in verbal expression.
3. To provide the child with activities to develop body and space awareness.
4. To provide ideas and guidance for preparing his/her own breakfast.
5. To provide information about a good breakfast.
6. To provide knowledge of the need for a good breakfast.
7. To provide reinforcement for eating a good breakfast.
8. To provide parent and child school experience.
9. To provide a sequential pattern for getting ready for the day.
10. To provide experience in setting a table.

Materials

Scissors
Doll
Crayons
9" x 12" white construction paper
Old magazines with pictures of breakfast items: juice, eggs, milk, yogurt, fruit, cold and hot cereal, bacon, French toast, pancakes, waffles, ham, toast, etc.
Paste
Paper Plates
Unit 4 Clothing Patterns
House Journal

Procedure

1. Reproduce Unit 4 Boy/Girl School Clothing (pages 98 and 99) on white paper. Make a few extras.

2. Give each child his/her clothing.

3. Have each child color and add designs to his/her clothing. Cut out the clothing on the heavy line and try it on the doll. Remember to give cutting assistance if needed.

4. Have each child put his/her name on the back of his/her clothing to eliminate confusion while playing together. Some children may need assistance with this task. Encourage them to copy their names from the back of the doll or envelope.

5. Have the children put the nightwear on their dolls and pretend they are getting up in the morning: brushing teeth, taking off P.J.'s/nighties, getting dressed in newly-made clothes, and eating breakfast.

6. Have the children make a list of good things to eat for breakfast.

7. Display pictures of good things to eat for breakfast on a chalk ledge. Pictures from the Peabody Kit and American Dairy Association are excellent. If duplicate pictures are available, allow the children to sort and match as a group activity or later as an individual activity.

8. Write an experience story about why we need breakfast. Help the children bring out ideas, such as: growth, strength, and thinking power.

9. Discuss whether there is someone available to prepare breakfast and whether the best breakfast foods are available. "I can eat cereal, toast, eggs, and even pancakes . . . to make my day start right." Chart the things the children say. Save the chart for review.

10. Have each child return doll and clothing to his/her envelope for storage after all activities.

Enrichment Activities

1. Make a chart with the children's names down the side and two school weeks across the top. Record with stickers or stars when they eat breakfast. Do this for a two-week period.

	Mon	Tues	Wed	Thurs	Fri	Sat
Sue	★		★		★	
Tom		★	★	★		
Mike	★					
Lee	★	★	★	★		

2. Have the children role-play preparing and eating breakfast with their dolls.

3. Show them how to cut apples into slices or rings and put peanut butter on them for a good breakfast or snack. Have them sample it too!

4. Have the children tell their paper dolls about their favorite breakfast.

5. Fingerplay:

   A. **BREAKFAST**

      Breakfast is good. (Rub tummy)
      Breakfast makes me grow. (Stand on tiptoes; reach arms high)
      Breakfast helps me think. (Touch head)
      So, I eat breakfast every day. (Pretend eating)

6. Have the children cut good breakfast items out of old magazines and paste them on paper plates.

7. Have the children prepare breakfast for the parents, making it a special occasion. Muffins, orange juice, milk, and baked eggs make a great menu. The muffin mixes, juice, eggs, ingredients, napkins, and plastic silverware and plates can be contributed by parents.

   The day before, prepare muffins from mixes, set the table, and mix the eggs together, storing them in the refrigerator in covered gallon plastic jugs.

20

Baked Egg Recipe

16 eggs, beaten

2 cups milk

1 teaspoon salt

1 teaspoon prepared mustard

1 cup grated Cheddar cheese

1/2 stick margarine

Mix eggs, milk, salt, and mustard and store. One-half hour before serving, melt margarine in a 9" x 13" pan in 325° oven. Tip pan so melted margarine covers pan. Pour in eggs; put cheese on top. Bake at 325° for 25 minutes, or until firm and just turning brown on top. Cut in squares.

Have at least four mothers or adults to help prepare and serve. This is fun!

8. Have each child set the table for one person. Practice placing the napkin on the left, the spoon and knife on the right, the glass at tip of the knife on the right, and the plate in the center.

9. Have the child draw a picture of a good breakfast in his/her personal journal. Have the child tell the teacher a story about a good breakfast. Record the story in the child's journal with or without the teacher's assistance.

10. Have the children take out the paper dolls, and then locate and name the following body parts of the doll: head, eyes, nose, mouth, hair, neck, body, legs, arms, feet, and hands. Then, repeating after the teacher, have the children locate and name the same parts on themselves, e.g., "This is my head. These are my eyes."

UNIT 5 - PARTY DAY

Goal

To practice getting ready for a party and to attend a party or similar event.

Objectives

1. To provide for exploration and development of coloring, cutting, manipulating, and creating.
2. To provide experience in verbal expression.
3. To provide activities to develop body and space awareness.
4. To provide practice in personal hygiene.
5. To provide practice in manners.
6. To provide cooking and party fun.
7. To introduce the technique of inviting someone to a party.

Materials

Scissors
Crayons
Doll
9" x 12" light blue construction paper
Unit 5 Clothing Patterns
House Journal

Procedure

1. Reproduce Unit 5 Boy/Girl Party Clothing (pages 100 and 101) on light blue paper. Make at least two or three extras.

2. Give each child his/her clothing.

3. Have each child color and add desired designs to his/her clothing.

4. Have the child cut out his/her clothing on the heavy line and try it on the doll. Remember his/her developmental age (Unit 1, Procedure 7).

5. Remind the children to put their names on the back of the clothes or help them with this task. Encourage them to try themselves.

6. Talk about getting ready for a party and keeping themselves clean. Discuss the need for baths and showers, washing and combing their hair, and brushing their teeth.

7. Have them role-play and get their dolls ready for a party, i.e., take a bath, wash the hair, and brush teeth. Allow time to make washcloths out of pieces of napkins for their dolls.

8. Have each child return the doll and clothing to his/her envelope for storage after all activities.

Enrichment Activities

1. Role-play by inviting someone else and his/her doll to a party. Make sure everyone has a partner. Example: Put different colors and shapes (these may be laminated) by pairs in a bowl and let the children find their matching partners. This is the person with the shape that matches theirs. This technique can be used over again.

2. Role-play and discuss manners.

   a. sitting down to eat
   b. "please pass the _____"
   c. "please" and "thank you"
   d. napkin in lap
   e. "no, thank you"
   f. not talking with food in mouth
   g. not filling the mouth too full

   Role-play with their dolls those things listed above. To help them remember, state the items and have the child repeat and role-play.

3. Have a tea party.

   a. Make gingerbread mix in a miniature cupcake pan to eat at the party. One regular mix for 24-30 cakes.
   b. Have the children bring their dressed paper dolls and sit in a circle. Reread or tell the children a version of The Gingerbread Boy.
   c. Have the children eat their gingerbread cakes.

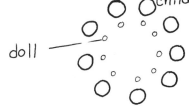

4. Fingerplay:

A. I'M A LITTLE TEAPOT

I'm a little teapot round and stout.

(Make hands and arms show round and stout, children standing)

Here is my handle, (Hand on hip)

Here is my spout. (Curve other hand out)

When I get all steamed up, then I shout.

Tip me over and pour me out. (Tip body toward hand with spout)

Here's a cup (Form cup with one hand)

And here's a cup (Form cup with other hand)

And here's a pot of tea. (Use both hands)

Pour a cup (Pouring motion)

And pour a cup

And have a drink with me. (Pretend to drink)

5. Write an experience story about making gingerbread cakes.

6. Have each child draw a picture in his/her personal journal about the tea party. Have the child tell the teacher a story about the tea party. Record the story in the child's journal with or without teacher assistance.

7. Give each child a 2" x 3" piece of colored paper. Have the children take their dolls and cover the body parts as directed.

Cover one arm	Cover one shoulder
" one leg	" one foot
" both arms	" ears
" both legs	" chest
" nose	" stomach
" both eyes	" hip
" mouth	" knee
" one hand	" elbow

8. With partners, have the children cover these listed parts on their dolls and take turns telling each other what is covered. Then let them choose what to cover. Allow them to do this for about five minutes.

24

UNIT 6 - SWIMMING

Goal

To develop understanding of the need for swimming safety.

Objectives

1. To provide exploration and development of coloring, cutting, manipulating, and creating.
2. To provide experience in verbal expression.
3. To provide activities to develop body and space awareness.
4. To provide the child with knowledge of swimming safety rules.
5. To provide knowledge of the importance of learning to swim.
6. To provide fun swimming.
7. To provide exposure to left and right.

Materials

Scissors
Crayons
Doll
9" x 12" white construction paper
6" x 6" piece of colored paper
Unit 6 Clothing Pattern
House Journal

Procedure

1. Reproduce Unit 6 Boy/Girl Swim Suits (page 102) on white paper. Make a few extras.

2. Give each child his/her clothing.

3. Have each child color and add desired designs to his/her clothing.

4. Have the child cut out the clothing on the heavy line and try it on the doll. Cutting assistance should be minimal after this unless children are very young.

5. Remind the children to put their names on the back of the clothes, helping those who need guidance.

6. Have each child make a beach towel and ball out of the colored paper.

7. Discuss swimming safety: not pushing others, splashing others, holding others under water, running, and knowing the rules of the lake or pool. Discuss why children should learn to swim. Write a class experience story about swimming after the discussion.

8. Make a pretend pool and diving board on the floor using masking tape about 3' x 4'. Make a walking ledge also. Have the children bring their dolls dressed in swim suits. Have 10 or 12 children at a time come and have a swimming party. Have them role-play swimming safety, pretending the dolls are having fun swimming and obeying the rules.

9. Have each child return the doll and clothing to his/her envelope for storage after all activities.

Enrichment Activities

1. Have each child draw a picture in his/her personal journal about swimming. Then have the child tell the teacher a story about swimming. Record the story in the child's journal with or without the teacher's assistance.

2. If the school has a pool, or if the weather is warm enough, visit the pool or lake for practice of good swimming manners.

3. Fingerplays:

A. THE LITTLE TURTLE

There was a little turtle,

He lived in a box,

    (Shape on hand palm up, fingers and thumb cupped up)

He swam in a puddle,

    (Use pointer finger of other hand as turtle;

    go around in palm of hand)

He climbed rocks.

    (Use same finger; climb up fingers of cupped hand)

He snapped at a mosquito,

    (Snap fingers of uncupped hand)

He snapped at a flea,

    (Snap fingers of uncupped hand)

He snapped at a minnow,

    (Snap fingers of uncupped hand)

He caught a mosquito,

    (Pull closed hand to chest)

He caught the minnow,

    (Pull closed hand to chest)

But he didn't catch me.

    (Point to self and shake head)

B. <u>FISHES</u>

Five little fishes
    (Hold up left hand)
Swimming in a pool,
    (Drop hand and wiggle fingers)
This one says,
"The pool is cool."
    (Hold up left hand; point with right pointer to left thumb)
This one says,
"The pool is deep."
    (Point to left pointer with right pointer)
This one says,
"I'd like to sleep."
    (Point to left tall finger with right pointer)
This one says,
"I'll float and dip."
    (Point to left ring finger with right pointer)
This one says,
"I see a ship."
    (Point to left little finger with right pointer)
Fisherman's boat comes,
Lines go--splash!
Away our five little fishes dash.
    (Clap hands on "splash")

C. TEN FINGERS AND TEN TOES AND ME

(Children point to parts of body as they repeat words.)

I have ten little fingers and ten little toes.
Two little arms and one little nose.
One little mouth and two little ears.
Two little eyes for smiles and tears.
One little head and two little feet.
One little chin--that's _____(Child's name)_____ complete.

4. Body awareness--touch different parts of the body of a gingerbread paper doll and say, "This is my head; touch your doll's head." Continue with:

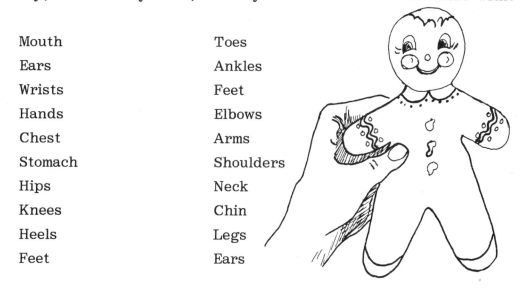

Mouth	Toes
Ears	Ankles
Wrists	Feet
Hands	Elbows
Chest	Arms
Stomach	Shoulders
Hips	Neck
Knees	Chin
Heels	Legs
Feet	Ears

Then have the children close their eyes and touch the same parts of their bodies as instructed by the teacher.

5. At this time it may be appropriate to say, "I did not ask you to touch the private parts (those parts covered by your bathing suit) on your doll, or even on yourself. Those are your private parts, and we do not let anyone touch those; nor do we touch others' private parts."

6. Have the children walk the funny feet with their dolls. Have the child touch the doll's left foot on his/her left foot and do the same with the right foot. The funny feet are 12 green feet with even numbers (2-24) and 12 red feet with odd numbers (1-23) applied to the floor with contact paper. The green feet are left feet; the red feet are right feet. The children say "left" as they step on the left foot and "right" as they step on the right foot. This activity also aids in the learning of odd and even numbers.

If young children have trouble with stepping with the correct foot, tape green circles on the left foot of the child and red circles on the right foot; help them walk it until they do not need assistance. Children enjoy this as an everyday activity. This is an activity that can be done without the doll. It could be experienced without the doll as a form of practice before using the doll.

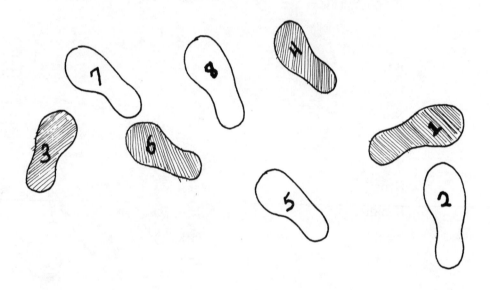

UNIT 7 - DENTIST AND TEETH

Goal

To develop and reinforce dental care and knowledge of the dentist as a helper.

Objectives

1. To provide exploration and development of coloring, cutting, manipulating, and creating.
2. To provide experience in verbal expression.
3. To provide activities to develop body and space awareness.
4. To provide knowledge about teeth.
5. To provide knowledge about dental care.
6. To provide reinforcement for good care of the teeth.
7. To provide an awareness of what a dentist and his/her hygienist do for children and their teeth.
8. To provide practice with the color white.

Materials

Scissors

Crayons

Doll

9" x 12" white construction paper

2" x 18" strip of colored construction paper

4" x 7" piece of white construction paper

Paste

Unit 7 Clothing Patterns

House Journal

Procedure

1. Reproduce Unit 7 Boy/Girl Outfit to go to Dentist (pages 103 and 104) on white paper. Make a few extras.

2. Give each child his/her clothing.

3. Have each child color and add desired designs to the clothing.

4. Have the child cut out the clothing on the heavy line and try it on the doll.

5. Remind them to write their names on the back of the clothing, helping those who need guidance.

6. Visit the dentist's office. Have the dentist/hygienist talk to the children about dental care. Have them show the children how to brush and floss their teeth.

7. When returning to the room, dress the doll in the clothes. Have the children role-play their visit to the dentist's office with their dolls. Each child plays the dentist, telling and showing the doll what the dentist told him/her.

8. Have the children write and send a group thank you note to the dentist/hygienist.

9. Write a class experience story about the visit to the dentist.

10. Talk about what teeth do for us, how they help us do this, and why we have teeth. Tell the children teeth are made of bone-like substance, are covered with enamel, and that you have two sets of teeth. Tell them your teeth chew, cut, and grind food.

Have the children make a big toothbrush out of 2" x 18" colored paper and 4" x 7" white paper. Use the colored strip as a handle and use the white paper for the bristles. Make bristles by cutting into the white paper about 1/8" apart and 2-1/2" in length; paste onto the handle. This makes a giant toothbrush. A very small one could be made out of scraps for the paper doll. Point out and talk about how the bristles and our teeth are white.

12. Put the children in groups of five. Have the children dress their dolls and pretend they are taking their dolls to the dentist. Have one of the children pretend to be the dentist or hygienist and clean the doll's teeth.

13. Have the children pretend to brush their teeth and tongue, plus floss their teeth. Have them use their small toothbrushes and brush their dolls' teeth, reminding them to brush up and down and around.

14. Make a chart like the breakfast chart (Unit 4, Enrichment 1) and use stars to indicate when the children brush their teeth. Check every day for a period of two weeks.

15. Have each child return the doll and clothing to his/her envelope for storage after all activities.

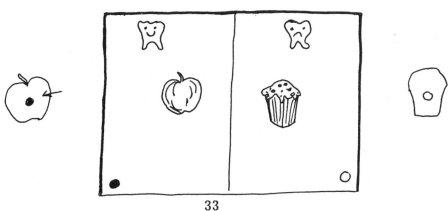

Enrichment Activities

1. Have a carrot, celery, and apple-eating party and talk about how these foods help clean your teeth when you cannot brush.

2. Game: "Happy Tooth-Sad Tooth"

   Begin with a 12" x 18" piece of tagboard (folded in the middle and laminated). Draw a "happy tooth" on the left side and a "sad tooth" on the right side. Laminate pictures of good and bad food. Use equal amount of good food and bad food pictures; about 12-14 would be sufficient. Code the good and bad food pictures with a colored circle on the back of each picture, such as: green on the back of the good food and red on the back of the bad food.

   Have the children place pictures of good food on the "happy tooth" side and place pictures of bad food on the "sad tooth" side. Also, place a green circle on the left side below "happy tooth" and a red circle on the right side below "sad tooth" of the game board. This will provide for self-checking.

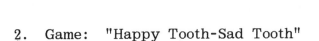

3. Fingerplay:

A. <u>BRUSH YOUR TEETH</u>

Brush, brush, brush your teeth

(Pretend to brush teeth up, down, and around)

Up and down, up and down, up and down,

Around and around and around.

Brush your tongue, brush your tongue

(Pretend to brush tongue up and down)

Brush your tongue, up and down.

Floss, floss, floss your teeth,

(Pretend to floss teeth, using both hands, back and forth)

To keep them clean and shiny.

4. Have the child draw a picture of a smiling mouth with white teeth in his/her personal journal. Then have the children tell the teacher the story about "Why We Need to Brush Our Teeth." Record the story in child's journal with or without the teacher's assistance.

5. Suggested reading:

<u>The Berenstain Bears Visit The Dentist</u>. Stan and Jan Berenstain. New York: Random House, 1981.

<u>How Many Teeth?</u>. Paul Showers. New York: Crowell Company, 1962.

6. The teacher says, "Touch your body with other body parts."

Nose to shoulder	Fingers to neck
Hands to knees	Elbow to back
Chin to ankle	Wrist to stomach
Toes to nose	Foot to other leg
Wrist to leg	Heel to other toe
Elbow to ear	Heel to other heel
Wrist to ankle	Hand to stomach

Now change it and have the child get out the doll and touch his/her nose to the doll's shoulder, his/her hand to the doll's knee, his/her chin to the doll's hip, etc.

UNIT 8 - FIRE FIGHTER AND FIRE STATION

Goal

To develop a respect and understanding of fire and fire fighters.

Objectives

1. To provide exploration and development of coloring, cutting, manipulation, and creating.
2. To provide experience in verbal expression.
3. To provide activities to develop body and space awareness.
4. To provide awareness of the danger of fire.
5. To provide knowledge of the fire fighter as a helper.
6. To provide knowledge of what to do when there is a fire.
7. To provide practice with the color red.

Materials

Scissors

Crayons

Doll

6" x 9" piece of red construction paper

9" x 12" piece of red construction paper

12" x 18" piece of red construction paper

Unit 8 Clothing Patterns

House Journal

Procedure

1. Reproduce Unit 8 Fire Fighter Clothing (pages 105 and 106) on 6" x 9" red construction paper for the hat and 9" x 12" red construction paper for the suit. Make a few extras.

2. Visit the fire station. Look at the trucks and talk to the fire fighters.

3. Discuss the way fire fighters are our helpers. They help and protect us. They fight fires and save lives. They have to be trained for their jobs. They have to know how to help injured people and how to rescue people. Show and tell the children how to get out of their houses if there is a fire. Either have the fire fighter talk about these matters, or the teacher should discuss them with the children.

4. Write and send a class thank you note to the fire department.

5. Give each child his/her clothing. It may be necessary to precut the inner line for the hat.

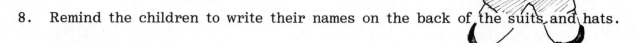
cut slip head in.

6. Have each child color details and write a number on the hat.

7. Have the child cut out the fire fighter's outfit on the heavy line and try it on the doll.

8. Remind the children to write their names on the back of the suits and hats.

9. Have each child return the doll and clothing to his/her envelope for storage after all activities.

10. Have each child write an experience story about the fire station and trucks.

Enrichment Activities

1. Make a fire truck out of 12" x 18" red construction paper. Talk about the truck being red. Some fire trucks are not red. Explain that since we want to learn the color red, today we are going to make ours red.

2. Talk about the consequences of: playing with matches and lighters; what to do if you see a fire; and how a firebox and fire extinguisher are used. Talk about how to get out of their houses in case of fire.

3. Put the fire fighter outfit on the paper doll and role-play with the doll how to get out of their houses if there is a fire.

4. Practice a fire drill taking the paper doll along.

5. Fingerplay:

A. TEN FIRE FIGHTERS

Ten brave fire fighters, (Hold up ten fingers)
Sleeping in a row, (Fingers curled)
Ding goes the bell, (Pretend ringing bell)
Down the pole they go. (Close fists and slide down)
Off on the engine (Pretend to drive truck)
Oh! Oh! Oh!

6. Have the child put the fire fighter's outfit on the doll and pretend to be a fire fighter going to a fire, helping people, and putting out the fire.

7. Show the children how to call the station. Have them learn the phone number. Allow the children to role-play with their dolls and call the fire station to report a fire.

8. Have the children draw pictures of a fire fighter in their personal journals. Then have each child tell the teacher the story "How The Fire Fighter Helps Us." Record in the child's journal with or without the teacher's assistance.

9. Suggested reading:
   I Can Be A Fire Fighter. Rebecca Hankin. Chicago: Childrens Press, 1985.

10. Have the children get out their dolls. Teacher asks them to touch doll's:

Head to floor	Head to table
Nose to window	Back to wall
Ear to chair	Front to wall
Shoulder to floor	Chest to desk
Elbow to chalkboard	Wrist to chalkboard
Knee to floor	Stomach to floor

Have them do the same with their own bodies.

11. Game: Body Parts

Play a game with the doll, touching child's:

   Back to doll's back
   Face to doll's face
   Heel to doll's heel
   Elbow to elbow
   Ankle to ankle
   Nose to nose
   Cheek to cheek
   Ear to ear

UNIT 9 - LIBRARY

Goal

To develop an awareness of the library as a source of enjoyment and knowledge.

Objectives

1. To provide exploration and development of coloring, cutting, manipulating, and creating.
2. To provide experience in verbal expression.
3. To provide activities to develop body and space awareness.
4. To provide a visit to the local library.
5. To provide knowledge about the care of books.
6. To provide exposure to the need for books.
7. To provide experience in turning pages in a book.

Materials

Scissors
Crayons
Doll
9" x 12" white construction paper
9" x 12" heavy brown paper
Unit 9 Clothing Pattern
House Journal

Procedure

1. Reproduce Unit 9 Jeans Clothing (page 107) on white paper. Make a few extras.

2. Give each child his/her clothing.

3. Have each child color and add desired designs to his/her clothing.

4. Have the child cut out the clothing on the heavy line and try it on the paper doll.

5. Remind the children to write their names on the back of their clothing, helping those who need guidance.

6. Plan a visit to the local library. Ask the librarian to tell the children a special story. Alert the librarian that the children might like library cards. This would be a good time for parents to go too. Let the children know that librarians are helpers.

7. Talk about school library rules and list them, i.e., care of books and importance of quietness. Tell them the same rules apply to the town library. Tell them they will need library cards to get books from the library.

8. Discuss that Saturday, while wearing our jeans, is a good day to visit the library. Explain that reading and looking at books helps us to learn many things.

9. Visit the local library. Upon returning to the school, have the children tell their dressed dolls about the visit to the library.

10. Make a list or chart about why we read and look at books.

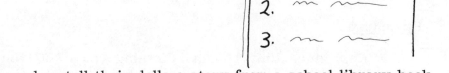

11. Have the children read or tell their dolls a story from a school library book.

12. Write and send a class thank you note to the library.

13. Have each child return the doll and clothing to his/her envelope for storage after all activities.

Enrichment Activities

1. Place a green line or small hand on left side of the child's desk or table place. Do the same with red on the right side. This helps children with concept of left and right and can reapplied over and over throughout the year. The child can practice going from left to right, when doing work and reading, by placing his/her left finger on the green line and walking it to the red line. The child can also walk the doll from the green line to the red line, going from left to right.

2. Have the children open the book on the desk or table and point out that the green line should have the spine or back of the book toward the green line. Have the children open the cover on the same side as the red line. This will help with how to open books and start at the front. Point out that this is starting at the front and reading from left to right.

3. Have the children trace their dolls on 9" x 12" heavy brown paper. Have the face and other designs colored on the doll. Have the duplicate doll cut up into a puzzle of six or seven parts and give it to a friend to put together. The puzzle could be kept by the friend or returned to the maker to put back together on a white paper.

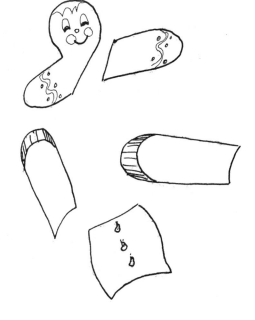

4. Fingerplay:

   A. A BOOK

      Here is a book. (Palms together)
      Let's open it wide, (Open hands up)
      And see the pages (Wiggle fingers to show pages)
      That are inside.

5. Have the children draw a picture in their journals about the trip to the library, and then tell the teacher a story about the trip. Record the story in the child's journal with or without the teacher's assistance.

UNIT 10 - BAKERY

Goal

To gain knowledge about and enjoy the bakery and the baker.

Objectives

1. To provide exploration and development of coloring, cutting, manipulating, and creating.
2. To provide the child with experience in verbal expression.
3. To provide the child with activities to develop body and space awareness.
4. To provide awareness of the bakery.
5. To experience baking cookies.
6. To develop awareness of how the baker is a helper.
7. To provide practice with the color brown.

Materials

Scissors

Watercolors

Doll

9" x 12" white construction paper

Unit 10 Clothing Patterns

House Journal

Procedure

1. Reproduce Unit 10 Boy/Girl Baker Clothing (pages 108, 109, and 110) on white paper. Make a few extras.

2. Talk about the bakery. Make a picture list of the things the children think the baker makes for us to eat and how we think he/she makes these things.

3. Visit the bakery. Have the children observe what is being made and how.

4. Make a new picture list of the things that they saw the baker make and compare this list with the first one. Have them notice how many things are <u>brown</u>.

5. Have the children make and send thank you pictures to the baker.

6. Have the children write an experience story about the bakery.

7. Give each child his/her clothing.

8. Have each child paint with watercolors to add desired designs to his/her clothing.

9. After the paint is dry, have the child cut out the clothing on the heavy line and try it on the paper doll.

10. Remind the children to put their names on the back of their clothing, helping those who need guidance.

11. Have the children make chocolate cake cookies. One recipe makes enough cookies for 24-30 children.

   <u>Chocolate Cake Cookies</u>

   1 chocolate cake mix (regular size)
   2 eggs
   1/2 cup oil

   Mix well and drop by teaspoons onto ungreased cookie sheet. Let the children mix and drop the batter. Bake at 350° for 10 minutes. Have them notice that they are <u>brown</u>.

12. Have the children tell and show their baker-dressed paper dolls how to bake cookies.

13. Let the children have a cookie for a treat.

14. Have each child return doll and clothing to his/her envelope for storage after all activities.

Enrichment Activities

1. Have the children make a big gingerbread doll. Enlarge the doll pattern, if necessary, using an opaque projector. Use tagboard to make a pattern about 36" long; this will be enough to make five patterns. Cut out the pattern and have the children trace it on heavy <u>brown</u> wrapping paper. Have the children cut it out. When cutting is completed, have them paint white frosting around the edges and paint a black raisin nose, eyes, buttons, and mouth.

2. Cut apart the pictures made in Procedures 2 and 4. Have the children match and sort likenesses and differences. Pictures could be laminated for use later on.

3. Have each child draw a picture in his/her journal about making cookies. Then have the children tell the teacher a story about the cookie-making. Record the story in the child's journal with or without the teacher's help.

4. Fingerplays:

   A. <u>PAT-A-CAKE</u>

      Pat-a-cake, pat-a-cake, baker's man, (Clap hands together)
      Bake me a cake as fast as you can, (Mix batter)
      Pat it and prick it (Clap hands, pretend to prick with pin)
      And mark it with a "B" (Make letter "B" in air)
      And put it in the oven
      For baby and me.

B. <u>DOUGHNUT HOLE</u>

Here is a doughnut, big and fat,

    (Make a circle with thumb and forefinger)

There's a hole in the middle, but don't eat that!

    (Point to hole)

5. The following recipe may be sent home to mom and/or dad:

<u>Gingerbread Girls and Boys</u>

1/2 cup shortening	1/2 teaspoon soda
1/2 cup sugar	3/4 teaspoon ginger
1/2 cup molasses	1/4 teaspoon nutmeg
1/4 cup water	1/2 teaspoon cinnamon
2 1/2 cups four	1/8 teaspoon allspice

Cream shortening and sugar. Blend in remaining ingredients. Cover. Chill 2-3 hours.

Preheat oven to 375°. Roll dough 1/4" thick on floured board. Cut out boys/girls. Place on ungreased baking sheet. Trim with raisins, cherries, string licorice, candies, and icing. Bake 10-12 minutes.

6. Have the children touch their body parts to environs. The teacher asks the child to touch:

Wall to wall	Ear to window
Hands to floor	Nose to table/desk
Elbows to chalkboard	Shoulder to floor
Head to floor	Fingers to books
Knees to floor	Chest to wall
Hands to table/desk	Wrist to chalkboard
Back to wall	Stomach to wall
Ankles to wall	

Repeat procedure and have the children touch their paper dolls' body parts to environs.

UNIT 11 - APPLE ORCHARD

Goal

To increase knowledge of how apples are grown by the farmer and how the apples get to the store.

Objectives

1. To provide exploration and development of coloring, cutting, manipulating, and creating.
2. To provide experience in verbal expression.
3. To provide activities to develop body and space awareness.
4. To provide practice with the color green.
5. To provide experience at an orchard.
6. To provide knowledge of the farmer as a helper.
7. To provide experience making applesauce.

Materials

Scissors
Crayons
Doll
Apples
9" x 12" white construction paper
9" x 12" red construction paper
Newsprint
Unit 2 Basic Clothing Pattern
Apple Journal

Procedure

1. Reproduce Unit 2 Basic Clothing Pattern Number 2 (page 93) on white paper. Make a few extras.

2. Give each child his/her blank clothing.

3. Explain that the children are to put apples (red, green, and yellow) all over their blank clothing. They can also add pockets, buttons, and anything else they desire. Show them red, green, and yellow apples; try to find them with leaves. Have each child add the desired designs. Give each child an apple to eat.

4. Have the children cut out the clothing on the heavy line and try it on their dolls. Also, remind them to put their names on the back of their clothing. They may want to make an apple out of scraps for their paper dolls.

5. Take the children to visit an apple orchard. It is especially interesting if the farmer will show them how to pick an apple and explain how apples grow and are delivered to the grocery store.

6. Write a class experience story about the visit to the orchard.

7. Have the children trace and cut out gingerbread dolls. Have them color and make apples in the dolls' hands. Staple the dolls' hands together in chain fashion and put a label on the string of dolls saying "We thank you for letting us come visit the orchard." This makes a great thank you for the farmer.

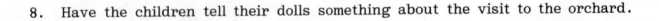

8. Have the children tell their dolls something about the visit to the orchard.

9. Have each child return the doll and clothing to his/her envelope for storage after all activities.

Enrichment Activities

1. Make applesauce:

    3/4 cup water
    12 medium apples
    3/4 cup sugar
    1/4 cup red hots

Wash, peel, and core apples; cut into quarters. Slice into two or three pieces and place in saucepan. Add water; cover. Cook over medium heat 10-15 minutes or until tender. Remove from heat; add red hots and sugar. Stir until red hots dissolve. Serves 24. (Allow children to cut up and stir apples, as appropriate.)

Have an applesauce-tasting party. Give each child a small disposable cup or bowl, a spoon, and two or three tablespoons of applesauce.

2. Using the Apple Journal Pattern (page 118), make a booklet shaped like an apple for each child. The booklet will be used for the rest of the stories in this book. Use two sheets of 9" x 12" red construction paper for the covers. Include ten pages of newsprint for the pages. Staple at the top and stem of the apple. Have each child decorate and write his/her name on the cover. Have the child draw an apple tree with apples on it in his/her journal. Have the children tell the teacher the story about "How Apples Grow On Trees" and record the story in their journals with or without the teacher's guidance.

3. Make a bulletin board of big apples painted with happy faces with glued-on leaves. Use paper at least 12" x 18". Precut apples may be used. Use wide brushes to paint the apples. Allow them to dry; then paint in the face and glue on the leaves. Put them on the bulletin board and label them "The Good Apple Bunch."

4. Emphasize the leaves on the apple trees are <u>green</u>. The leaves the children make are <u>green</u>.

5. Have different colors and sizes of apples. Allow the children to sort them according to size and color. Place them in plastic baskets and use them as a free-time activity until apples are no longer usable. You might use three red apples, four yellow apples, and two green apples as color matching. Use four little apples, two big apples, and five medium apples.

6. Fingerplays:

A. <u>APPLE TREE</u>

Away up high in the apple tree,
    (Hold hands above head, form circles
    with thumb and forefinger of each hand)
Ten red apples smiled at me. (Smile)
I shook that tree as hard as I could,
    (Put hands out as if on tree; shake)
And down they came (Hands above head; drop to ground)
1, 2, 3, 4, 5, 6, 7, 8, 9, 10.
And mmmmmmmmmm were they good! (Pat stomach)

B. <u>HAPPY ME</u>

Two eyes to see nice things to do. (Point to eyes)
Two lips to smile the whole day through. (Point to mouth)
Two ears to hear what others say. (Point to ears)
Two hands to put the toys away. (Hold up hands)
A tongue to speak sweet words each day. (Point to tongue)
A loving heart for work or play. (Put right hand on heart)
Two feet that errands gladly run. (Point to feet)
Make happy days for everyone. (Smile)

7. Say and have the child fill in:

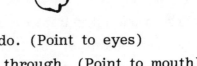

I see with my _____.	I shrug with my _____.
I smell with my _____.	I twist with my _____.
I talk with my _____.	I jump with my _____.
I snap with my _____.	I run with my _____.
I walk with my _____.	I hop with my _____.
I clap with my _____.	I write with my _____.
I wave with my _____.	

8. Read <u>Mr. Bump</u> by Roger Hargreaves.

UNIT 12 - HAIR CARE

Goal

To expand cognizance of hair care.

Objectives

1. To provide exploration and development of color, cutting, manipulating, and creating.
2. To provide experience in verbal expression.
3. To provide activities to develop body and space awareness.
4. To provide awareness of the barber/hairdresser as a helper.
5. To provide knowledge of how to wash, brush, and comb hair.
6. To provide practice with the color black.

Materials

Scissors

Crayons

Doll

9" x 12" white construction paper

24" x 36" black construction paper

12" x 18" drawing paper

Old magazines with pictures of hair

Paste

Unit 1 Basic Clothing Patterns

Apple Journal

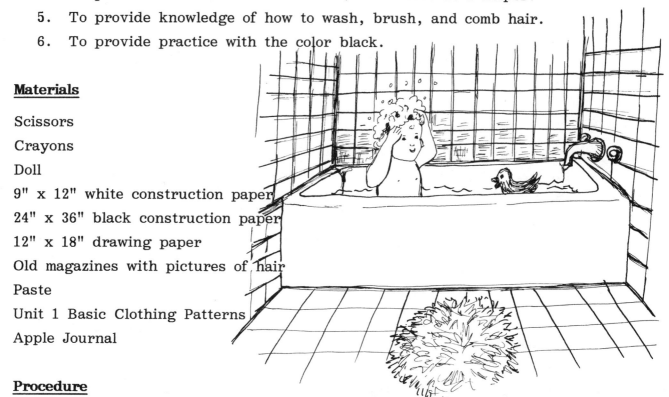

Procedure

1. Reproduce Unit 1 Boy/Girl Basic Clothing Pattern 1 (pages 91 and 92) on white paper. Make a few extras.

2. Give each child his/her clothing and the piece of black paper. Give each child two raisins to copy. Have the child cut five raisins out of the black paper and eat the real raisins. Tell the children they are going to be able to paste the (paper) raisins on their dolls' clothes.

3. Have each child color and add desired designs and raisins to his/her clothing.

4. Have the child cut out his/her clothing on the heavy line and try it on the paper doll.

5. Remind the children to write their names on the back of their clothing, helping those who need guidance.

6. Have a barber/hairdresser come to visit and show the children how to wash and brush their hair. They could tell the children why and how we get our hair cut.

7. Have the children write a class experience story about what the visitor told them.

8. Have the children write and send a class thank you note to the barber/hairdresser.

9. Cut out pictures of all basic hair colors: black, blond, brown, and red (include all races). Paste hair colors at the top of the 24" x 36" paper. Divide the paper into at least five columns. Let each child cut out a head of hair from a magazine. Then have them paste the hair in the appropriate column. After the chart is completed, discuss likenesses and differences on the chart.

10. Have each child return the doll and clothing to his/her envelope for storage after all activities.

Enrichment Activities

1. Give each child a 12" x 18" piece of drawing paper. Have the child take out his/her paper doll and trace around it. Have the children color the tracing and add lots of hair.

2. Have the children take out the paper dolls and clothes. The teacher may have to pattern a response the first time.

CLOTHES WE WEAR

Teacher	Children's Response	
Hold up a coat	"This is a coat"	
" hat	" hat	
" dress	" dress	
" pants	" pants	
" shirt	" shirt	
" swim suit	" swim suit	
" P.J.'s	" P.J.'s	
" nightie	" nightie	

3. Have each child draw a picture and write a story in his/her journal about "Taking Care Of Your Hair."

4. Fingerplay:

   A. MY HAIR

      This is my hair. (Touch hair)
      This is the way I wash my hair. (Pretend to wash hair)
      This is the way I brush my hair. (Pretend to brush hair)
      Don't I look nice? (Smile)

5. Use an old pair of white cotton dress gloves that fit your hands. Color all of the left glove with a green permanent marker and write "left" on the front of it in black. Color all of the right glove with a red permanent marker and write "right" on the front of it in black. Use these gloves to practice left and right. These activities can be used over and over.

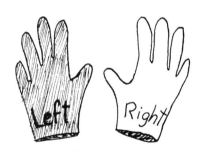

   a. Put the gloves on with your back to the children. Raise the left hand, saying "left." Raise the right hand, saying "right."

   b. Put the gloves on with your back to the children. Raise and wave the left hand, saying "left." Raise and wave the right hand, saying "right."

c. Put the gloves on and stand behind each child, saying "left"; touch his/her left hand with your gloved left hand. Do the same using the right hand and glove.

d. Let the child put on the gloves, wave the right hand, and say "right." Do the same with the left hand.

UNIT 13 - DOCTOR AND NURSE

Goal

To increase the awareness of the doctor and nurse as care givers.

Objectives

1. To provide exploration and development of color, cutting, manipulating, and creating.
2. To provide experience in verbal expression.
3. To provide activities to develop body and space awareness.
4. To provide positive interaction with a doctor and/or nurse.
5. To provide an awareness of women being doctors and men being nurses.

Materials

Scissors

Crayons

Doll

9" x 12" white construction paper

12" x 18" black construction paper

1" x 3" red construction paper

Cotton balls, cotton swabs, tongue depressors, and plastic bandages

Unit 13 Clothing Patterns

Apple Journal

Procedure

1. Reproduce Unit 13 Nurse/Doctor Clothing (pages 111, 112, 113, and 115) on white paper. Make a few extras.

2. Visit a doctor's office or have a doctor or nurse come to visit. Have the doctor/nurse tell the children:
    a. They go to school for many years to become doctors and nurses.
    b. There is much to learn about ways to keep people well.
    c. Doctors can do many things for us.
    d. Nurses assist them to help us.
    e. Hospitals also help the doctor. They have special equipment to help people.
    f. Nurses work in hospitals too.

3. Have the children see the film strip <u>Say Ah</u>, People Who Work, Beginning Concepts, Unit 1, Scholastic Magazine, Inc. Englewood Cliffs, NJ. The film depicts a woman doctor in her professional role and in her family role. If this is not available to show, talk to the children about women being doctors while still being mothers and grandmothers. The teacher could also discuss the concept of men as nurses, fathers, and grandfathers.

4. Have the children write a class experience story about how the doctor/nurse is our helper and how they take care of us when we are sick.

5. Give each child his/her clothing. Point out that the nurse has a girl's outfit and the doctor has a boy's outfit. But, a woman can be a doctor and a man can be a nurse.

6. Have each child color and add desired designs to his/her clothing.

7. Have each child cut his/her clothing on the heavy line and try it on his/her paper doll.

8. Remind the children to write their names on the back of their clothing.

9. Have the children role-play the doctor and the nurse helping us to keep well.

10. Have the children tell their paper dolls how the doctor and the nurse help us.

11. Make and send a happy face mural to the doctor/nurse. Have the children make happy faces, write their names on them, and paste them on a large piece of paper. The teacher may write "thank you" on the mural.

12. Have each child return the doll and clothing to his/her envelope for storage after all activities.

Enrichment Activities

1. Have the children make a chart of how they can help themselves and others keep well. Help them to become aware of (include on the chart): washing hands, not putting things in their mouths (except food), and covering their mouths when they sneeze or cough. Have the children illustrate the chart after completion.

2. Have the children draw pictures and write stories in their journals about "How To Keep Well."

3. Make a doctor's bag by using a 12" x 18" piece of black construction paper and the "doctor's bag" pattern. Fold the black paper and place the cut-out pattern on the fold. Trace and cut it out. Use the pattern for the two handles, trace them, and cut them out. If the children are capable of doing this themselves, allow them to do so. For younger children, cut out the pieces. Have them staple the sides and paste on the handles and a red cross. A red cross can be made from two 1" x 3" red strips. Give each child one cotton ball, two cotton swabs, three tongue depressors, and four plastic bandages to count, sort, and put in the bag. Have the children dress their dolls in Unit 13 Clothes and, using their doctor's bag, play as if they are doctors.

4. Suggested reading:
   Curious George Goes To The Hospital. Margaret and R. A. Rey. Boston, MA: Houghton Mifflin Co., 1966.
   I Can Be A Doctor. Rebecca Hankin. Chicago: Childrens Press, 1984.

5. Repeated because of the need for reinforcement. Practice left and right with gloves. (Refer to Unit 12, Enrichment Activities, number 5.)

6. Fingerplay:

A. TEN LITTLE FINGERS

I have ten little fingers and they all belong to me.
   (Hold up ten fingers)
I can make them do things, would you like to see?
   (Wiggle fingers)
I can shut them up tight, or open them wide.
   (Close hands tight and open wide)
I can put them together or make them hide.
   (Put fingers together; put hands behind back)
I can make them jump high,
   (Raise hands high; wave)
I can make them jump low,
   (Lower hands; wave)
I can fold them up quietly and hold them just so.
   (Fold hands; put in lap)

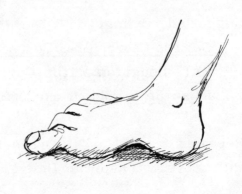

7. Parts of the body (teacher may have to pattern response initially).

Teacher	Children's Response
What do we use to pick things up?	Hands
What parts do we use to hear?	Ears
What parts do we use to stand?	Feet and legs
What parts do we use to jump?	Legs and feet
What part of the body do we use to smell?	Nose
What part of the body do we use to bend over?	Head and neck
What part of the body is at the end of our hands?	Fingers
What part of the body is at the end of our feet?	Toes

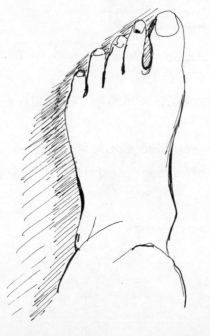

UNIT 14 - POLICE OFFICERS

Goal

To increase understanding of police officers as helpers to keep our neighborhoods safe places to live.

Objectives

1. To provide exploration and development of color identification, cutting, manipulating, and creating.
2. To provide experience in verbal expression.
3. To provide activities to develop body and space awareness.
4. To provide positive interaction with a police officer.
5. To provide a greater awareness of the danger of strangers.
6. To provide for the extension of knowledge about safety.
7. To provide practice with the color blue.
8. To provide awareness of shapes.

Materials

Scissors

Crayons

Doll

9" x 12" blue construction paper

6" x 9" blue construction paper

6" x 15" black construction paper

6" x 6" red, green, and yellow construction paper

Paste

Gold stars (one for each child)

Unit 14 Clothing Patterns

Apple Journal

Procedure

1. Reproduce Unit 14 Police Officer Clothing (pages 106 and 114) on blue paper; uniform on large sheet, hat on the smaller sheet. Make a few extras.

2 Discuss with the children:
   a. Police officers are symbols of authority and care.
   b. Police officers help keep our neighborhoods safe places to live and play.
   c. Laws are made to protect people, and the officer's duty is to see that the laws are enforced.
   d. Police officers also help us if we are lost or someone bothers us.

59

3. Invite a local police officer to visit the classroom. Ask him/her to cover these areas:

   a. How and where to ride bikes correctly and safely.

   b. Safety practices to follow when walking, watching for cars and signs, and cooperating with the safety patrols.

   c. The need to go straight home from school.

   d. An awareness of not talking to, going with, or accepting presents from anyone without parents' permission.

   e. His/her police car, if it is available.

   f. His/her uniform and firearm safety (weapons are not toys and should not be touched by children).

4. Give each child his/her clothing and one gold star. Point out the blue color of the clothes.

5. Have each child color and add desired designs to his/her clothing. Have the child place the gold star on the hat above the bill.

6. Have each child cut out his/her clothing on the heavy line. It might be helpful to cut out the bill line on the hats for the children.

7. Remind the children to put their names on the back of their clothing.

8. Have the children write a class experience story about the police officer's visit.

9. Have each child make a badge out of a 6" x 6" piece of yellow paper and write or copy his/her name on the badge. Staple the badges together forming a chain. Make a sign at the beginning that says "Thank you, Officer _____ " and send it to him/her on blue paper. Emphasize that the thank you is on <u>blue</u> paper.

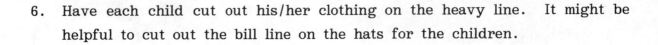

10. Dress the paper doll in the blue police officer's clothing and role-play being the police officer.

11. Have each child return the doll and clothing to his/her envelope after all activities.

Enrichment Activities

1. Game: Police Officer! Police Officer! My Child Is Lost!

   The teacher chooses a child to be the police officer. The police officer leaves the room. Another child is chosen to the "lost" child and hides. The police officer returns to the room. The class says, "Police officer! Police officer! My child is lost! Who is it?" The police officer gets three chances to guess who is missing. The one who was missing then becomes the police officer. The police officer then chooses the next lost child. The game continues in this manner for as long as desired.

2. Have the child draw a picture of a police officer and write a story in his/her journal about the police officer.

3. Make a traffic light.
   a. Give each child a piece of 6" x 15" black construction paper.
   b. Have the children trace red, green and yellow circles 4" across. Use the Winterhaven small circle templates or templates made from tagboard. Supply one template and a 6" x 6" piece of construction paper of each color for each child. Have the children cut out the circles after tracing them.
   c. Have them paste the circles on the black rectangle. Emphasize rectangle, circle, top, middle, and bottom. Have the children paste the red circle on the top, yellow in the middle, and green on the bottom.
   d. Explain to the children: when the light is red, it means stop; when the light is yellow, it means caution; and when the light is green, it means go.

61

4. Fingerplay:

A. BRAVE POLICE OFFICERS

We are brave police officers standing in a row. (All standing)

Sometimes we are tall, (Sometimes full upright)

Sometimes we are small. (Bend down)

Sometimes we are very, very tall, (Raise arms; stand on tip toes;
stretch tall)

Sometimes we are very, very small. (Bend down, close to floor)

Sometimes tall, sometimes,

See how we are now. (Sit down)

5. Suggested reading:

I Can Be A Police Officer. Catherine Matthias. Chicago: Childrens
Press, 1984.

UNIT 15 - DAIRY FARM, MILK AND BUTTER

Goal

To emphasize and gain knowledge about the farm and how cows give milk.

Objectives

1. To provide exploration and development of coloring, cutting, manipulation, and creating.
2. To provide experience in verbal expression.
3. To provide activities to develop body and space awareness.
4. To provide exploration of a dairy farm.
5. To provide experience of seeing cows milked.
6. To provide visualization of the milking process.
7. To provide awareness of what cows and calves eat.
8. To provide firsthand experience with making butter.

Materials

Scissors

Crayons

Doll

9" x 12" white construction paper

6" x 9" yellow construction paper

Unit 15 Clothing Patterns

Apple Journal

Procedure

1. Reproduce Unit 15 Farmer Clothing (pages 115 and 116) on white paper and Farmer's Hat on yellow paper. Make a few extras.

2. Visit a dairy farm. Ask the farmer to:
   a. Allow the children to feed or watch cows/calves being fed.
   b. Allow the children to see a cow milked.
   c. Allow the children to see what happens to the milk as it goes into a bulk tank.
   d. Explain that the milk is cooled in the bulk tank and then drained into large milk tank trucks. The milk truck takes the milk to plants where it is prepared and put into bottles and cartons for us to drink.

3. After returning to the classroom, have the children write an experience story about their trip to the farm.

4. Give each child his/her clothing.

5. Have each child color and add the desired designs to his/her clothing.

6. Have each child cut out the clothing on the heavy line and try the clothes on the paper doll.

7. Remind the children to write their names on the back of their clothing.

8. Have the children draw a picture of cows being milked and write stories in their journals about milking the cow.

9. Make copies of all the journal stories and put them all together. Make a cover out of colored construction paper. Write "Thank you, Mr. Farmer" on the cover and send it to the farmer as a thank you.

10. The children can put the farmer outfits on their dolls and role-play milking and feeding the cows and calves.

11. Each child can return his/her doll and clothing to the envelope for storage after all activities.

Enrichment Activities

1. Have the children make butter:
   a. Use three pint jars with a tight screw-on lid.
   b. Pour one cup of heavy cream in each of the pint jars with 1/8 teaspoon of salt. Screw on the lids very tightly.
   c. Divide the class into three small groups. Have each group sit in a circle.
   d. Give each group a jar. Have each child shake the jar 10-15 times and pass it on to the next child. Have them continue to pass it around the circle until the cream turns to butter. (There will be some remaining liquid left around the formed butter.)

e. Remove the butter from the jars and spread it on salted soda crackers for the children to taste. Have at least one or two crackers for each child. This recipe should be enough for at least 25-28 children.

2. Make cow puzzles. Have each child draw a cow picture on a 9" x 12" piece of paper. Have each child put his/her name on the back of the picture. Laminate the pictures or cover the front and back with clear contact paper. Have the children cut their puzzles into eight pieces. They can share their puzzles with a partner and put each other's together. Give them 6" x 9" envelopes to take their puzzles home.

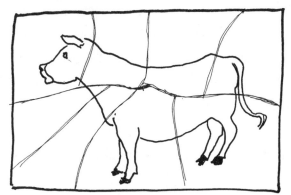

3. Sing a version of "Old MacDonald Had A Farm."

Old MacDonald had a farm, E-I, E-I, O,
And on that farm he had a cow, E-I, E-I, O.
With a moo, moo here, and a moo, moo there,
Here a moo, there a moo, everywhere a moo, moo,
Old MacDonald had a farm, E-I, E-I, O.

And on that farm he had a sheep, I-I, E-I, O.
With a baa, baa here, and a baa, baa there,
Here a baa, there a baa, everywhere a baa, baa,
Old MacDonald had a farm, E-I, E-I, O.

And on that farm he had a pig, E-I, E-I, O.
With an oink, oink here, and an oink, oink there,
Here an oink, there an oink, everywhere an oink, oink,
Old MacDonald had a farm, E-I, E-I, O.

And on that farm he had a dog; with a bow wow....

And on that farm he had a horse; with a heee heee....

And on that farm he had a chicken; with a cluck, cluck....

And on that farm he had a donkey; with a hee haw....

And on that farm he had a goat; with a blat, blat....

And on that farm he had a cat; with a meow, meow....

4. Fingerplay:

   A. LITTLE COW

   This little cow eats grass. (Hold up thumb)
   This little cow eats hay. (Hold up pointer)
   This little cow drinks water. (Hold up tall finger)
   This little cow runs away. (Hold up ring finger)
   This little cow does nothing but sleep all day--Lazy Cow!
        (Hold up little finger)

5. The teacher says, "Touch these parts of your body."

Head	Mouth	Body
Feet	Legs	Hands
Chin	Arms	Ears
Nose	Eyes	Fingers
Hair	Lips	Thumb
Neck	Waist	Shoulders

Have the children take out their dolls and put them in front of them with the dolls' feet toward their chests. Have each child touch the above body parts on the doll as directed by the teacher.

6. Place the doll in the same position as in number 5.

Teacher asks the children, "What do they do?"	Children respond verbally and touch the part of the doll
Knees	Bend Legs
Neck	Bend head
Elbows	Bend arms
Hips	Bend legs
Ankles	Bend feet
Wrists	Bend hands
Waist	Bend body

7. Ask, "What part is this?" Teacher asks and touches part on a paper doll;
child responds by touching the part on his/her own body. Start at the head.

Hair	Neck	Arms
Eyes	Shoulders	Hands
Nose	Chest	Fingers
Mouth	Back	Hips
Chin	Waist	Legs and feet

Then have the children take out their dolls and touch the parts as the
teacher says them.

UNIT 16 - STONE SOUP AND GROCERY STORE

Goals

To develop understanding of a grocery store and the grocer as a helper.

To develop insight into sharing while making and enjoying soup.

Objectives

1. To provide exploration and development of coloring, cutting, manipulating, and creating.
2. To provide experience in verbal expression.
3. To provide activities to develop body and space awareness.
4. To expose the students to different kinds of vegetables.
5. To provide exposure to buying groceries.
6. To provide practice in working and sharing together.
7. To provide practice in manners.

Materials

Scissors

Crayons

Doll

9" x 12" white construction paper

Unit 2 Basic Clothing Pattern

Apple Journal

Procedure

1. Reproduce Unit 2 Basic Clothing Number 2 (page 93) on white paper and make a few extras.

2. Read the folk tale <u>Stone Soup</u> by Marcia Joan Brown. Or, tell the story of how three hungry soldiers came to a village and showed them how to make stone soup by first putting a stone in a big kettle of boiling water. A great feast can be shared by all of the village when all contribute; adding vegetables, meat, and barley to the kettle.

3. List on paper all things added to "Stone Soup." Include stone, meat, cabbage, carrots, onions, corn, tomatoes, potatoes, celery, beans, peas, and barley.

4. Give each child his/her clothing. Have the children make a "Stone Soup" outfit. Suggest they add pockets; perhaps an apron and even some vegetables to their outfits. Have each child color and add desired designs to his/her clothing.

5. Have the children cut out their clothing on the heavy line, write their names on the back, and try the clothing on the paper dolls.

6. Make and eat some "Stone Soup" using the following procedure:

   a. Post the list made from the story.

   b. Have each child bring <u>one</u> item from the list with the adaptations for numbers. This recipe serves 25 children.

   1 clean stone
   1 soup bone
   4 potatoes
   6 carrots
   1/2 cabbage
   2 onions
   6 stalks celery
   1 can green beans
   1 can corn
   1 can peas
   4 tomatoes
   1 cup barley
   Salt and pepper to taste

   c. Have each child take home a note listing the items (including a spoon and bowl) to bring and the day he/she is to bring them.

   d. Visit the grocery store a day or two before making the soup to buy fruit, cookies, and crackers to eat with the soup. Have the children contribute to this cost, if desired. Talk about what we can buy and how to act in the grocery store. Walk through the grocery aisles to look at areas and items.

e. Plan to make the soup in the morning, or the day before if the children only attend half a day. Let the children cut up the potatoes, carrots, celery, onions, and tomatoes. Cook the raw vegetables, barley, and salt for about an hour over medium heat. After it comes to a boil, add canned vegetables and once again bring to a boil. Cook over medium heat for 15 minutes.

7. While sharing the soup, discuss table manners, such as: passing food, saying "please" and "thank you," not talking with food in the mouth, and remaining seated while eating.

8. After eating the soup and cleaning up, have the children dress their dolls and tell them about the soup.

9. Have the children write an experience story about making the soup.

10. Have each child return the doll and clothing to his/her envelope for storage after all activities.

Enrichment Activities

1. Carrot and Potato Relay:

Four containers will be needed for this game. Also, provide enough paper carrots and paper potatoes for each child (one carrot or potato per child). Divide the paper vegetables into two containers (one container for each team). Put the two empty containers on the opposite side of the room.

Divide the children into two teams. When it is each team player's turn, he/she will take a vegetable out of the container and, while carrying his/her doll, will carry the vegetable across the room and put it in the empty container. They cannot drop their dolls or vegetables on the way or they must start over. They cannot take their vegetables out until the preceding child has put his/her vegetable in the empty container. The first team to empty its container wins.

2. Fingerplay:

   A. <u>MR. CARROT</u>

   Nice Mr. Carrot
   Makes curly hair, (Circular motion over head)
   His head grows underneath the ground (Thumb pointed down)
   His feet up in the air. (Point up)
   Early in the morning
   I find him in his bed.
   I give his feet a great big pull, (Pull up)
   And out comes his head!
      (Arms akimbo, i.e., hands on hips, elbows turned outward)

3. Have each child draw a picture and write a story about visiting the grocery store in his/her personal journal.

4. Have each child trace around half of a paper doll. Then put the doll away and fill in the missing parts.

UNIT 17 - OUR HOUSE AND FAMILY

Goal

To develop an awareness of the likenesses and differences in our families and homes.

Objectives

1. To provide exploration and development of coloring, cutting, manipulating, and creating.

2. To provide experience in verbal expression.

3. To provide activities to develop body and space awareness.

4. To provide an opportunity to create houses and observe their likenesses and differences.

5. To provide an atmosphere of positiveness about each child's family.

Materials

Scissors

Crayons

Doll

Medium size cardboard box

Wallpaper books

2 sheets of 18" x 24" colored construction paper

Paste

Apple Journal

Procedure

1. Have each child make a doll house following this plan:

    a. Collect a box for each child from a local grocery store and cut out two windows and a door.

    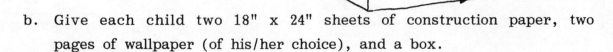

    b. Give each child two 18" x 24" sheets of construction paper, two pages of wallpaper (of his/her choice), and a box.

72

c. Have the children color or make the furniture, walls, and rugs out of colored paper, designing as they desire. Let them use wallpaper for the walls, curtains, and for anything else they wish. They may like to use crayons and/or magic markers to draw in flowers, grass, and trees on the outside of their houses. Help them develop many ideas for the house creation.

2. After the houses are completed, let the children take their envelopes and dolls and place them in the houses. Have them play house with their dolls. Encourage the children to play with others and suggest playing neighbors.

3. Have the children make a class chart of why their houses are alike and different. Store the houses to use later.

HOUSES	
Alike	Different

4. Use a large sheet of paper for a class mural. Have each child paint a picture of a house in a space 20" wide. The next day give them each as many circles as there are people in their families. Have them draw faces on the circles and paste them near their houses. After they paste faces on the paper, have them color the rest of the bodies.

5. Discuss families as being special because they help each other. Talk about how they help each other. How does Mom Help? Baby? Grandma? Grandpa? Aunt? Dad? Uncle? Brother? Sister? Have each child tell the teacher and have the teacher record his/her house picture "My family is good at _____ and _____ together as a family."

My family is good at making popcorn.

Enrichment Activities

1. Suggested reading:

   <u>The Terrible Thing That Happened At Our House</u>.   Marge Blain.
   New York: Scholastic, Inc., 1975.

2. Ask the children, "How do you help at home?" Have them role-play ways they help. Encourage caring, sharing, and supporting.

3. Have the children draw pictures of something they do to help at home and write stories in their journals about the pictures.

4. Make houses from lunch milk cartons. Wash out the cartons <u>very</u> well. Staple them together at the top to form a roof. Frost with icing and press on graham crackers to form house siding. Use icing as a glue to put on small candies and raisins for desired exterior. Eat or retain as desired.

5. Fingerplays:

   A. <u>TWO LITTLE HOUSES</u>

      Two little houses closed up tight,
      Open up the windows and let in the light.
      Ten little fingers, people tall and straight,
      Waiting for the kindergarten at half-past eight.
      (Procedure: Close fists for house, open for windows,
               hold up fingers for ten children)

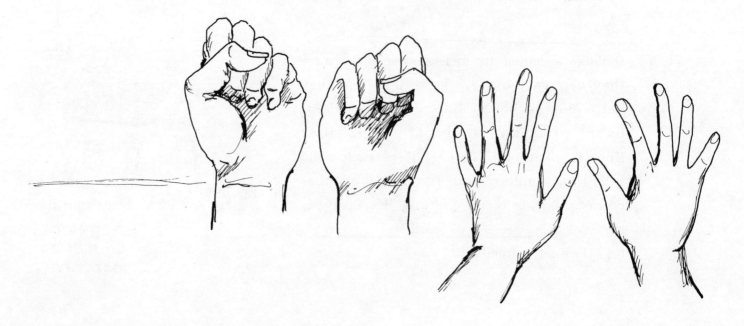

B. JIMMY'S HOUSE

Here is a house for Jimmy
    (Fold fingers of one hand over other fist)
And here's his yard for play.
    (Make big circle with arms)
Here is the mother who cares for the house
    (Point to thumb of left hand)
And the Daddy who works every day.
    (Point to forefinger)
The sister likes to help mother.
    (Point to middle finger)
The brother and Jimmy help too.
    (Point to ring and little fingers)
Their home is a place where they are happy and safe
    (Fold fingers of one hand over fist of other)
And they love their home just as you do.

C. TWO LITTLE MEN

Two little men lived in two little houses.
    (Show two fists)
One little man came out of his house.
    (Pull thumb out of fist)
He looked up the street and down the street.
    (Point up and down with thumb)
He didn't see anything, so he went back to his little house.
    (Put thumb in fist again)
The second little man came out of his house.
    (Repeat with other hand)
He looked up the street and down the street.
    (Point up and down with thumb)
He didn't see anything, so we went back in the little house.
    (Put thumb in fist again)
Then both little men came out of their houses.
They looked up the street and down the street.
    (Point up and down with thumb)
They didn't see anything so they went back into their little houses,
And stuck their heads out the windows.
    (Stick thumbs out between fingers)

6. Have the children take out their dolls and clothing. The teacher asks the children to:

   a. Dress the doll to go swimming.
   b. Dress the doll to go to bed.
   c. Dress the doll to go to school.
   d. Dress the doll to go out to play.
   e. Dress the doll to go to a party.
   f. Dress the doll for a cold day.

7. Review with a green left glove and a red right glove. The teacher can put the gloves on and have the children raise their right hand as the teacher raises her right hand. Have the children touch the following with their right hand: eyes, nose, mouth, ear, neck, leg, and stomach, as asked. Change and do the same with their left hand.

UNIT 18 - HALLOWEEN

Goal

To create Halloween enjoyment.

Objectives

1. To provide exploration and development of coloring, cutting, manipulating, and creating.
2. To provide experience in verbal expression.
3. To provide activities to develop body and space awareness.
4. To provide introduction and development of the skill to design paper doll clothing.
5. To provide practice with the color orange.
6. To provide exploration of the relationship of shapes and road signs.
7. To provide review of safe walking practices.

Materials

Scissors

Crayons

Pencils

Doll

12" x 18" white construction paper

5" x 5" orange construction paper

Apple Journal

Procedure

1. Illustrate the making of clothing to the children. Use the chalkboard and dolls. Trace around the dolls (except the head, hands, and feet). Remove the dolls after tracing. Fill in the lines at the end of the arms and feet and across the neck. Some children may wish to stop at the skirt line or extend the line to make pants or a long dress. Show them how to lay their dolls back on and add feet for shoes and hands for gloves. Add things to hold in their hands and add hats to their heads. Have them take out their dolls and practice on the chalkboard. Explain the necessity of tabs.

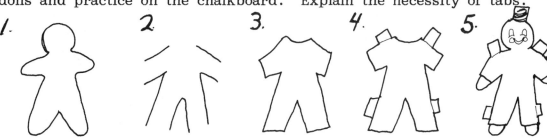

2. Tell the children they are going to make Halloween costumes. Make pictures and/or a word list of at least ten costume ideas.

3. Give each child a piece of 12" x 18" white construction paper.

4. Have the children get out their dolls, scissors, crayons, and pencils.

5. Instruct the children to create, design, and color the Halloween costumes they want to make for their dolls.

6. Observe the children making their clothing and give assistance when needed.

7. If the level of difficulty seems too high for the development of the child, provide and reproduce either of the two basic clothing patterns (pages 91, 92, and 93).

8. After completion, have the children cut out the clothing and try it on their paper dolls.

9. Remind the children to put their names on the back of their clothing.

10. Have each child make an <u>orange</u> pumpkin. Give each child a 5" x 5" piece of orange construction paper. Have the children trace or make a 4" circle on the paper. Have them draw a face on the pumpkin with a black crayon. Let them cut stems out of scrap green construction paper. Have the children put their pumpkins in their paper dolls' houses.

11. Discuss trick-or-treating safely, wearing light-colored clothing, clothing that does not cover their eyes, walking safely, and not eating treats until they get home so an adult can check the treats.

12. Write an experience story about how to walk on roads and streets safely. Encourage them to consider the following: walking against the traffic; wearing light-colored clothing after dark; watching street lights; looking both ways when crossing the street; and not talking to strangers.

13. Have the children dress the dolls in their costumes, get out their houses, and role-play trick-or-treating safety.

14. Have each child return the doll and clothing to his/her envelope after all activities.

Enrichment Activities

1. Have the child draw a picture of his/her costume and write a story in his/her journal.

2. Fingerplays:

   A. <u>JACK PUMPKIN FACE</u>

   Little Jack Pumpkin Face
   Lived on a vine.
   Little Jack Pumpkin Face
   Thought it was fine.

   First he was small and round,
       (Make small circle with hand)
   Then big and yellow.
       (Make circle larger)
   Little Jack Pumpkin Face
   Is a fine fellow.

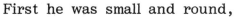

B. FIVE LITTLE JACK-O'-LANTERNS

Five little jack-o'-lanterns sat upon a gate.

Said the first little jack-o'-lantern,

"My, it's getting late."

Said the second little jack-o'-lantern,

"I hear a noise."

Said the third little jack-o'-lantern,

"It's just the boys."

Said the fourth little jack-o'-lantern,

"We'd better run."

Said the fifth little jack-o'-lantern,

"It's just Halloween fun."

Ooo-ooo-ooo-ooo went the wind,

Out went the lights,

And away they all ran on Halloween night.

C. WOULD YOU SHAKE?

Would you shake? (Child shakes)

Would you quake?

Would you say --

Oh! Goodness sake!

If a jack-o'-lantern jumped out at you

And said -- BOO! (Child jumps and says "Boo!")

3. Discuss and make road signs and shapes.
Examples: octagon (stop sign), triangle
(yield), circle (railroad), square
(direction). Have the children draw or
trace templates for shapes on 12" x 18"
white construction paper and complete
signs. Completion can include coloring
and adding sign posts. Words can be
added, such as "Stop," if the child is
able and wishes to do so.

4. As an alternative activity, each child could make a shape book with a shape
and a sign for each page. Include: oval, square, diamond, circle, triangle,
rectangle, and octagon.

5. Game: Silly Question

Have the children respond "yes" or "no" to the following:

Do chests smell?
Do eyes see?
Do hairs run?
Do arms jump?
Do necks turn?
Do ears hear?
Do tongues taste?
Do elbows eat?
Do teeth fly?
Do fingers bend?
Do teeth chew?
Do mouths eat?
Do legs hop?
Do legs hear?

UNIT 19 - BALLOONS

Goals

To increase, in a unique way, an awareness of distance.

Objectives

1. To provide exploration and development of coloring, cutting, manipulating, and creating.
2. To provide experience in verbal expression.
3. To provide activities to develop body and space awareness.
4. To provide practice with the color purple.
5. To provide practice in designing paper doll clothing.
6. To provide awareness of the postal service.
7. To provide the joy of watching a balloon ascending.

Materials

Scissors
Crayons
9" x 12" purple construction paper
Pencils
Doll
Balloons
Self-addressed postcards
Apple Journal

Procedure

1. Show the children how to make their own doll clothing. Use the chalkboard and dolls. Trace around the dolls (except the head, hands, and feet). Remove the dolls after tracing. Fill in the lines at the end of the arms and feet and across the neck. Some children wish to stop at the skirt line or extend the line to make pants or a long dress. Explain how and where to place tabs.

2. Explain to the children they are going to make balloon outfits. They are going to send up purple balloons. Show them an inflated purple balloon. Make a picture or written list on the chalkboard of things that could be drawn on the clothing. List five to seven items.

3. Distribute pieces of 9" x 12" purple construction paper. Emphasize <u>purple</u> paper. Ask them to say "purple" three times.

4. Have the children get out their dolls, scissors, crayons, and pencils.

5. Instruct the children to create, design, and color their clothing on the purple paper.

6. Tell them, "Tomorrow we will send up balloons, so we need super balloon outfits."

7. Observe the children making their clothing and give them assistance when it is needed.

8. Provide and reproduce either of the two basic patterns, if necessary.

9. After completion of the clothing, encourage the children to dress their dolls and play with them.

10. Send purple helium balloons up with attached self-addressed laminated postcards. Label the postcards "Please return to me," using a ballpoint pen. Have one for each child. It is exciting to see where the balloons go. When the cards return through the mail, explain how the mail carrier helps us get things from a distance.

11. Have the children write a class experience story about sending up the balloons.

12. Have the children return the dolls and clothing to their envelopes for storage after all activities.

Enrichment Activities

1. Have the children draw pictures and write stories in their personal journals about what happened to their balloons.

2. Have the children make purple balloons out of the scraps from the clothes. Attach strings to the paper balloons to create paper doll balloons.

3. Fingerplays:

A. A BALLOON

This is a little balloon. (Form small circle with hands)
This is a middle-sized balloon. (Hands wider apart)
This is a big balloon. (Hands very far apart)
POP! BANG! There goes the balloon. (Clap hands together)

B. PUFF, PUFF

Puff, puff, puff, (Blow)
I blow up my balloon (Form balloon with hands)
Puff, puff, puff, (Blow)
I knew it would break soon. (Clap hands)

4. Have the children lay their dolls face up on the desk. Have them touch parts of the body as the teacher says them:

Eyes	Stomach	Feet
Nose	Hair	Chest
Arms	Mouth	Head
Legs	Hands	Elbow and knees

Have the children turn the dolls face down and touch either the green or red lines or hands on desk or table, touching the green when you say "left" and red when you say "right." Repeat three times.

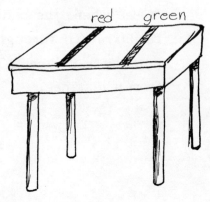

Then have the children touch the left arm of the doll, right arm of the doll, left leg of the doll, and right leg of the doll.

Show them that when they hold the doll with the back to their chest, the doll is facing the same way they are, and the doll's left side is the same as theirs, etc.

5. Hang up a long clothes line. Supply a large basket of <u>clip-on</u> clothes pins. Let three or four children hang clothes on the line. They could be asked to hang only school clothes, only community helper clothes, only jackets, only swim suits, only sleep cloths, and only party clothes.

6. Extended enrichment: Have the children take their doll clothing and houses home.

UNIT 20 - MATH ACTIVITIES

Goal

To reinforce the number values, recognition, and set relationship of 1 through 10.

Objectives

1. To provide a creative way to discover and learn numerals, their value, and set relationships 1 through 10.

2. To provide a reusable tool for experiencing and learning numerals, their value, and set relationships 1 through 10.

Materials

1. Two sets of 10 laminated gingerbread dolls with paper raisins for buttons. Start with 1 raisin button, going to 10 buttons. Use original doll pattern. Color code each set by putting a red dot on the back of each doll.

2. One set of 10 laminated gingerbread paper dolls with the numerals 1 to 10 on them. Use original doll pattern. Color code the set by putting a blue dot on the back of each doll.

3. One set of 10 laminated paper candies with numerals 1 to 10. Color code the set by putting a yellow dot on the back of each candy.

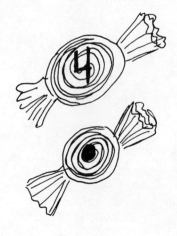

4. Raisins and napkins.

86

Procedure

1. Place correct number of real raisins on the dolls (set with raisins). Count while placing them on the buttons. Depending on the development of the child, it may be best to give each child only two or three dolls at a time to complete this task.

2. Give each child a napkin with a numeral on it. Have the children count out and place the corresponding number of raisins on the napkin. Then let the children eat the raisins.

3. Have the children use raisin button paper dolls and numeral candy sets. Have the children count the raisins on the raisin dolls and place the appropriate candy numeral on each raisin paper doll.

4. Match two sets of raisin button paper dolls--1 to 1, 2 to 2, and so on, to 10.

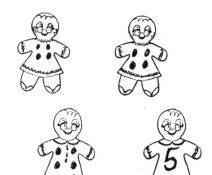

5. Match one set of raisin button paper dolls to corresponding and appropriate numeral paper doll.

6. Match numeral candy set to numeral paper doll set.

7. Use listed activities over and over to reinforce concepts.

UNIT 21 - COLOR AND THE GINGERBREAD BOY

Goals

To expand practice with colors.
To re-explore the story of The Gingerbread Boy.

Objectives

1. To provide experiences with colors.
2. To provide additional exploration of The Gingerbread Boy story.
3. To provide creative expression.

Materials

The Gingerbread Boy story
2" x 2" colored construction paper (red, blue, green, brown, orange, purple, yellow,
    white, and black)

Procedure

1. Read The Gingerbread Boy story at the beginning of this book. Ask the children to listen for color words and raise their hands when they hear them.

2. Give each child a 2" x 2" square of red, blue, green, brown, orange, purple, yellow, white, and black construction paper. Have them lay the squares in front of them.

3. Reread The Gingerbread Boy. As the story is read, have the children raise the corresponding colored square as they hear it.

4. Have the children pantomime the story as it is told.

5. Have the children make a play out of the story.

Girl Doll

90

Boy Doll

91 Basic Clothing Pattern Number 1
Girl's

92   Basic Clothing Pattern Number
Boy's

93   Basic Clothing Pattern Number 2

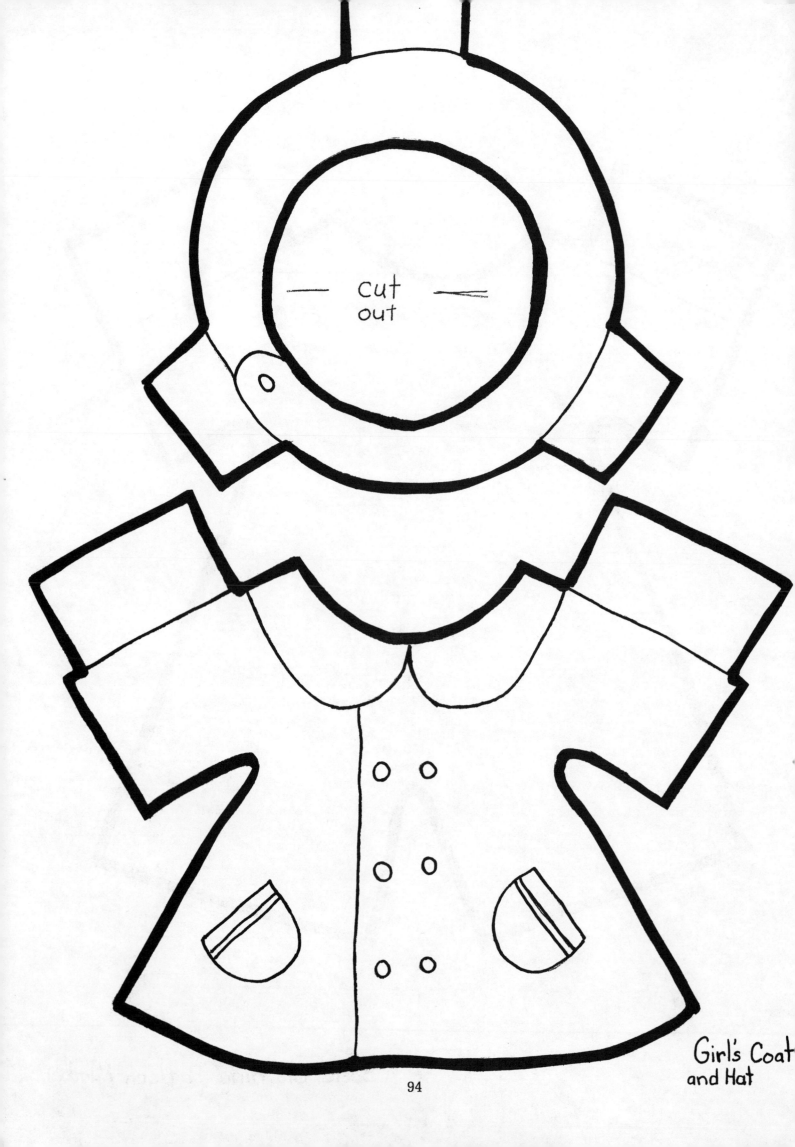

cut
out

94

Girl's Coat
and Hat

Boy's Coat and Hat

Girl's Night Clothes

Boy's Night Clothes

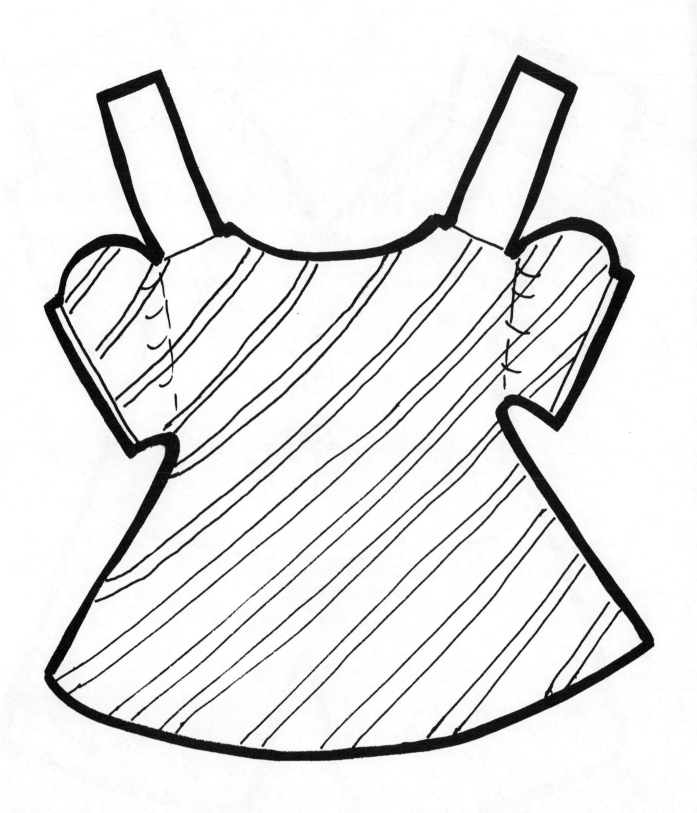

Girl's School Clothin

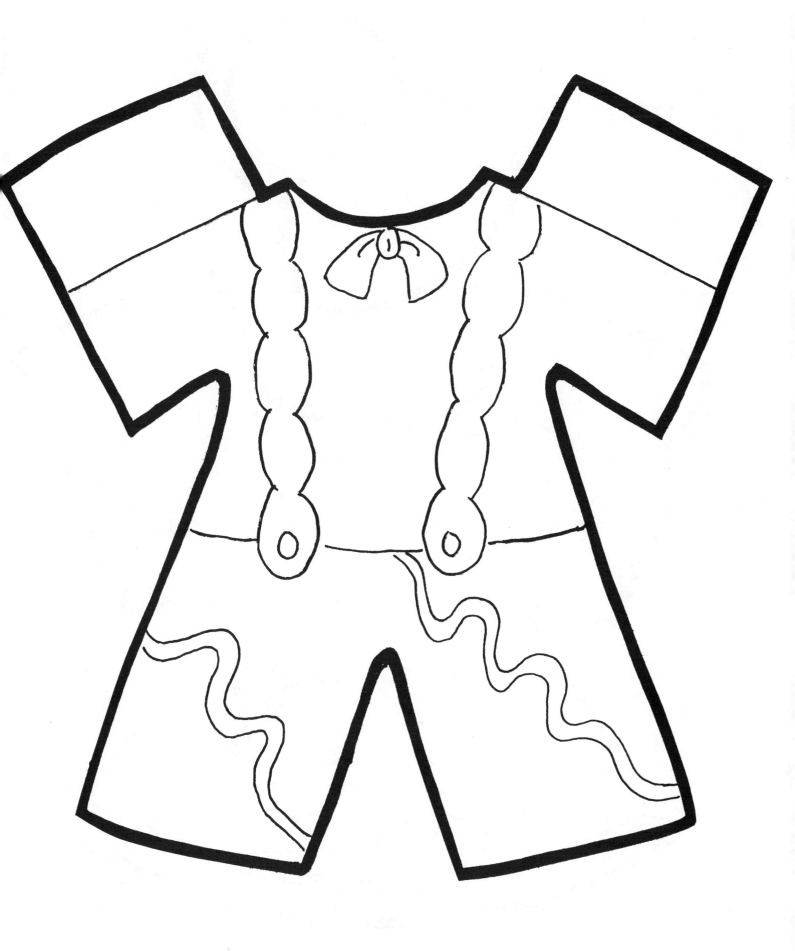

Boy's School Clothing

cut

Girl's Party Clothing

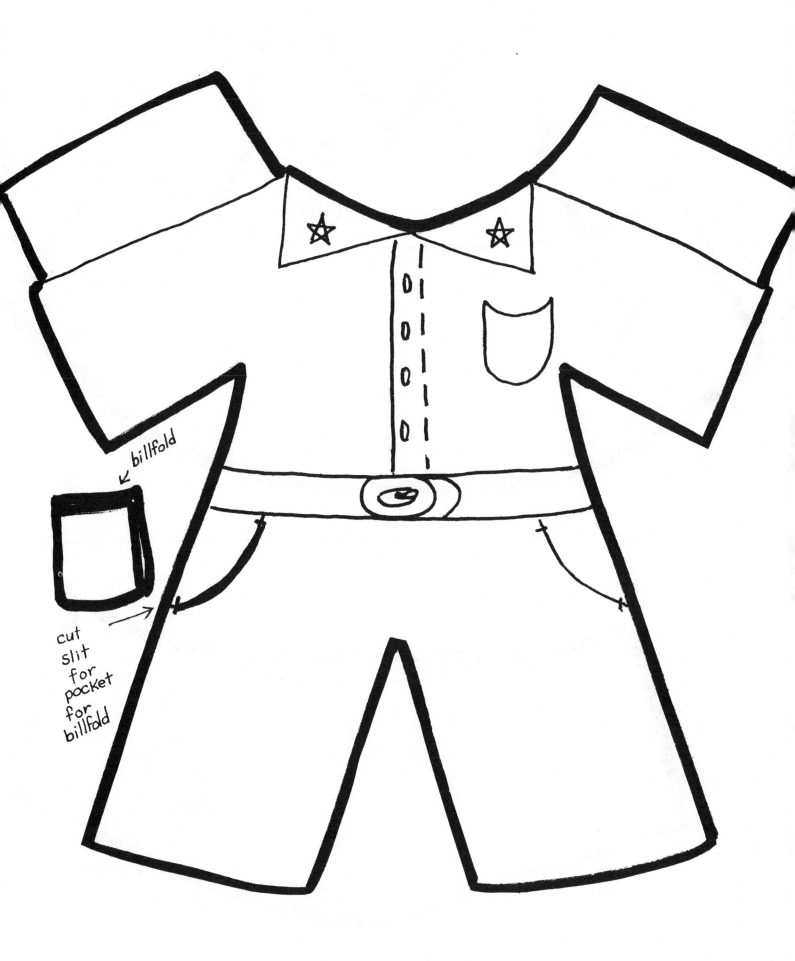

billfold

cut
slit
for
pocket
for
billfold

Boy's Party Clothing

I ♥

I love you

Swim Suits

Girl's Outfit to go to
Dentist

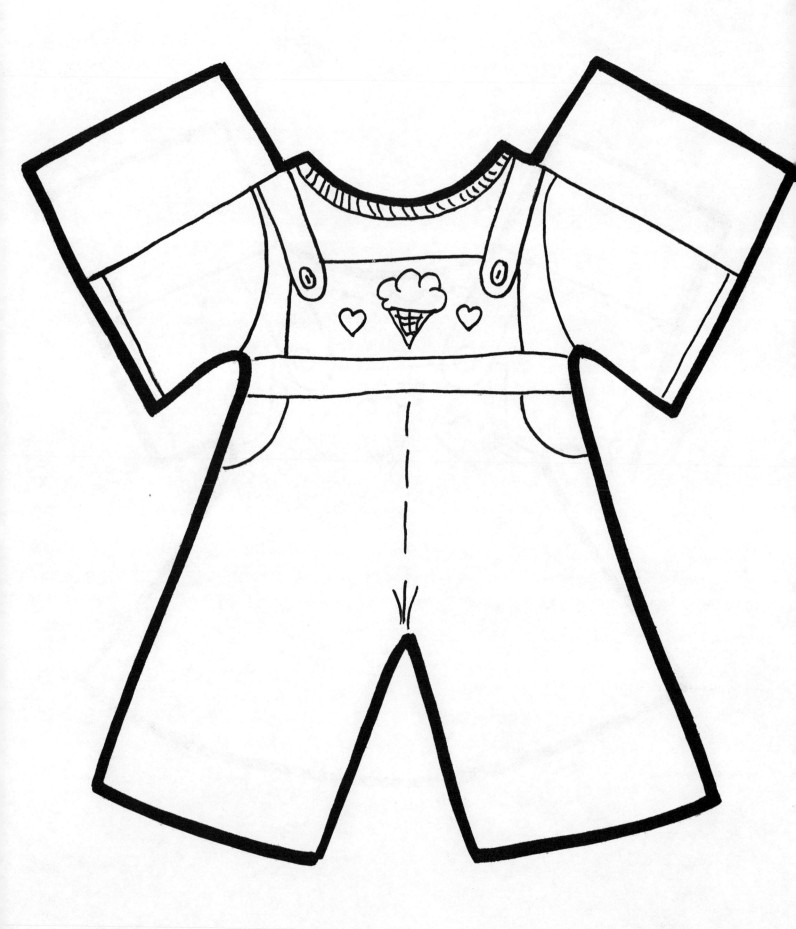

Boy's Outfit to go to
Dentist

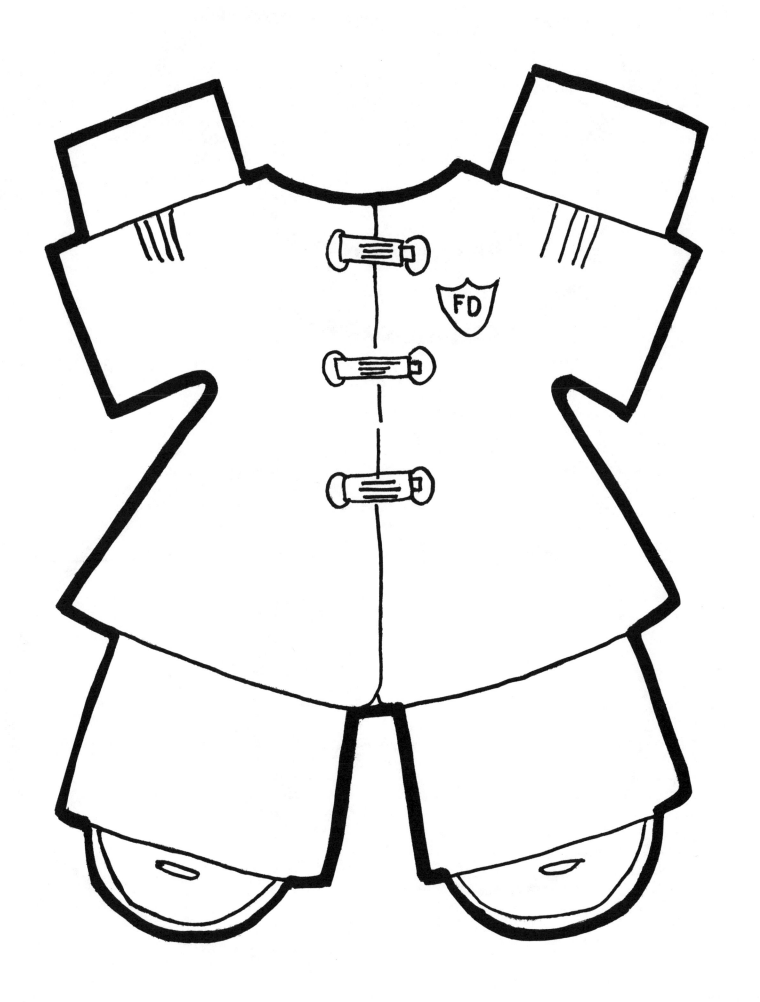

Fire Fighter Clothing

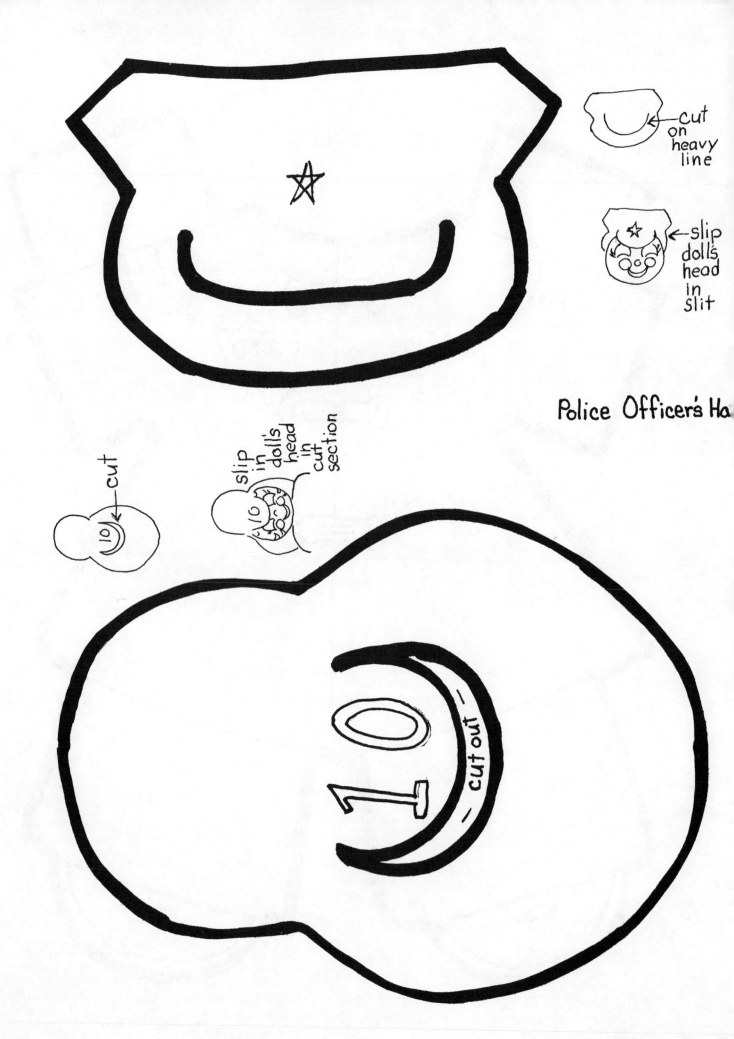

cut
on
heavy
line

slip
doll's
head
in
slit

Police Officer's Ha

cut

slip in doll's head in cut section

cut out

Fire Fighter's Hat

Mom ♡s me

design can be
covered and
have children
make their
own emblem

Jeans Clothing

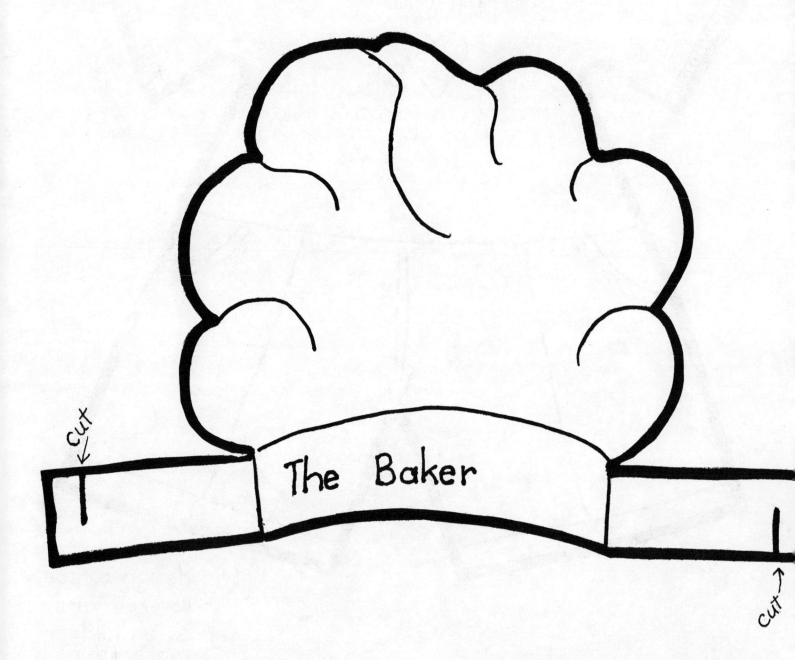

cut

The Baker

cut

Baker's Hat

Girl's Baker Clothing

Boy's Baker Clothin

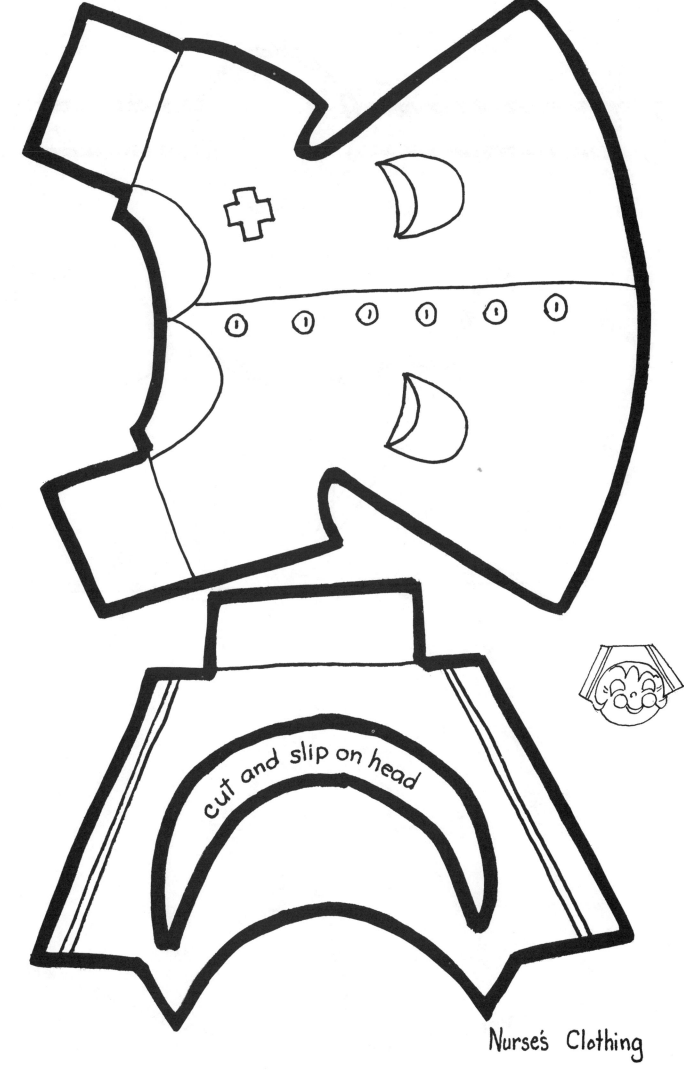

cut and slip on head

Nurse's Clothing

cut

cut

Doctor's Clothing

112

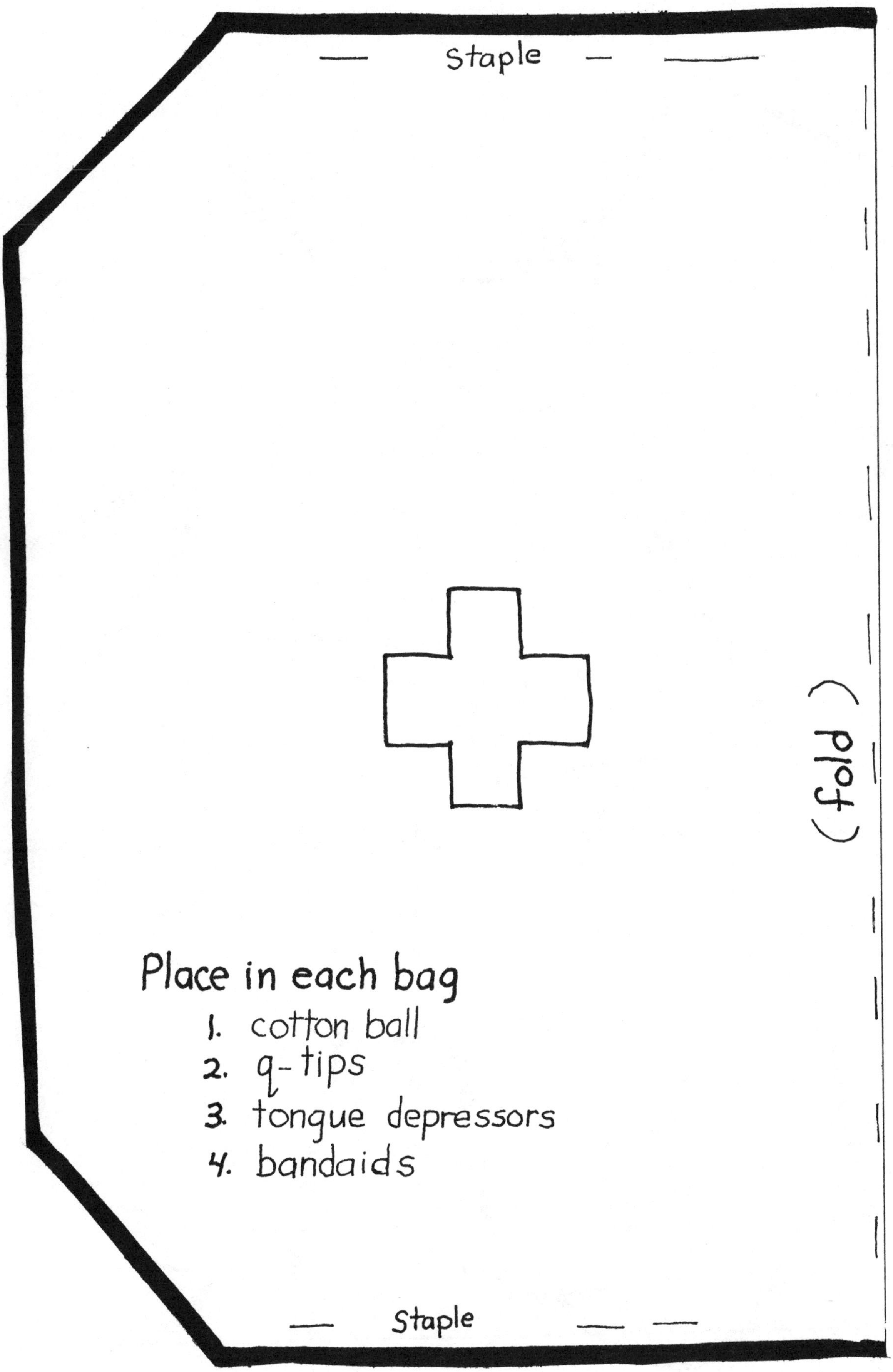

Staple

(fold)

Place in each bag
1. cotton ball
2. q-tips
3. tongue depressors
4. bandaids

Staple

Doctor's Bag

Police Officer Clothing

114

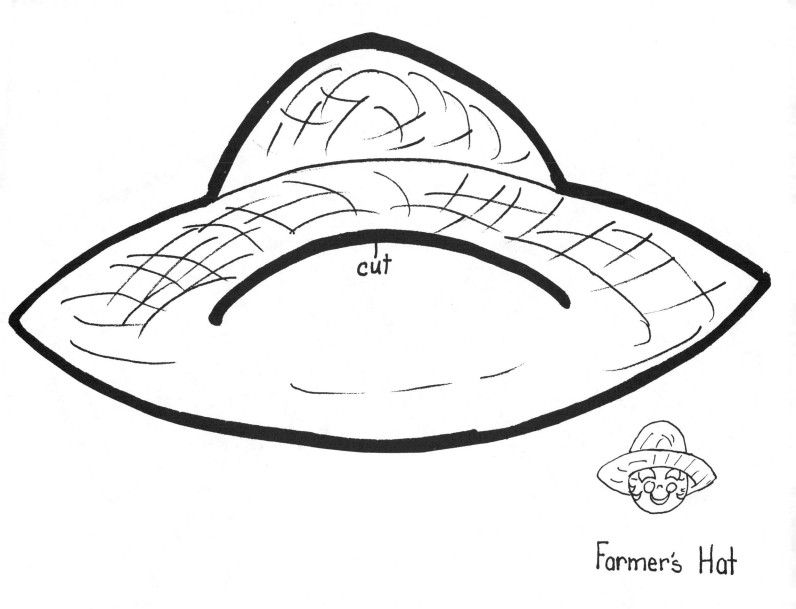

cut

Farmer's Hat

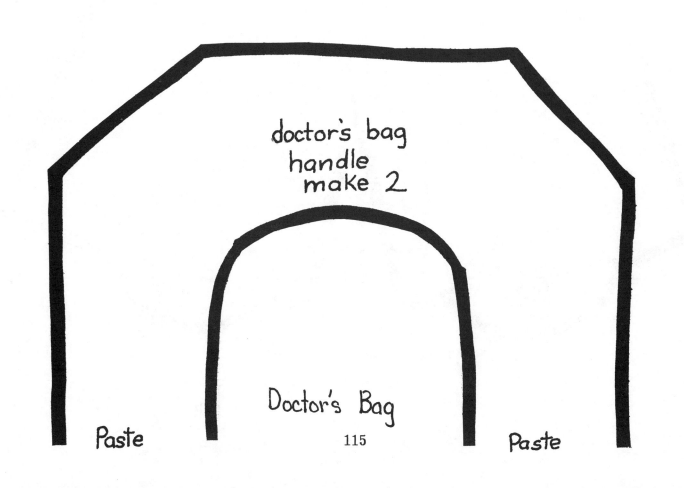

doctor's bag
handle
make 2

Doctor's Bag

Paste

115

Paste

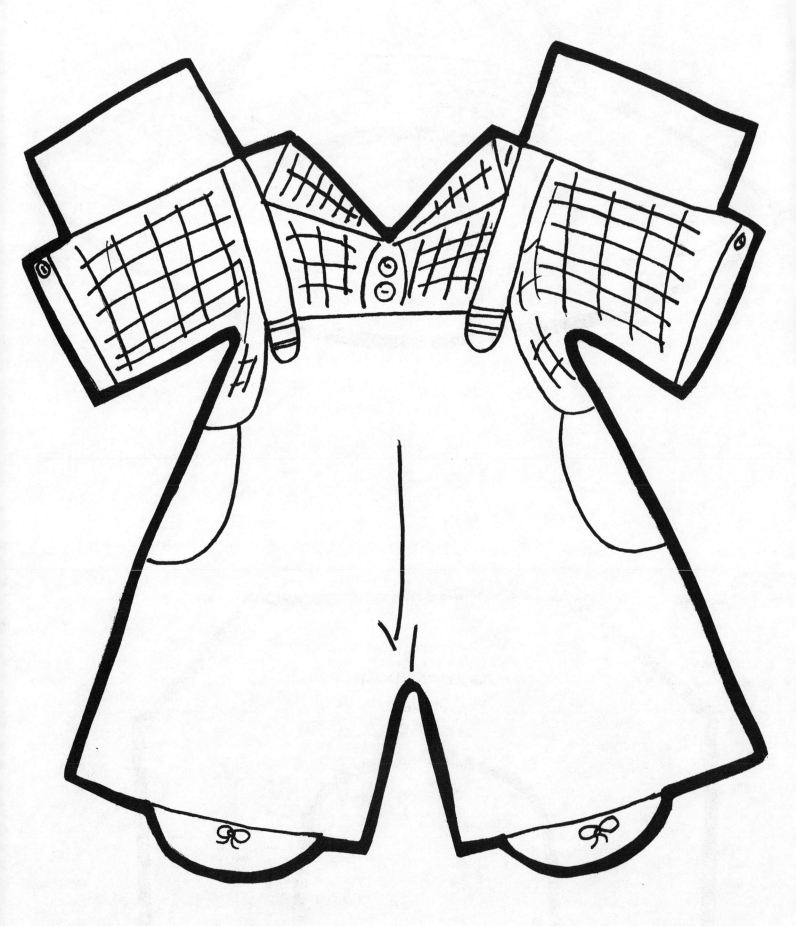

Farmer Clothing

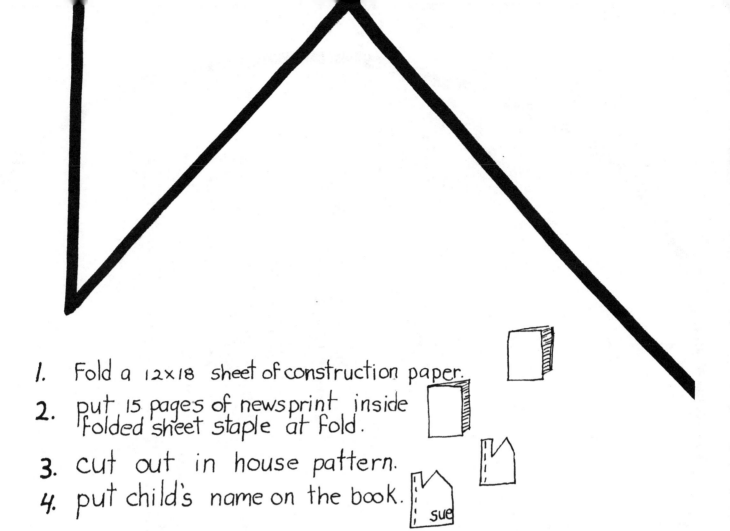

1. Fold a 12×18 sheet of construction paper.

2. put 15 pages of newsprint inside folded sheet staple at fold.

3. cut out in house pattern.

4. put child's name on the book.

Staple

House Journal
Pattern

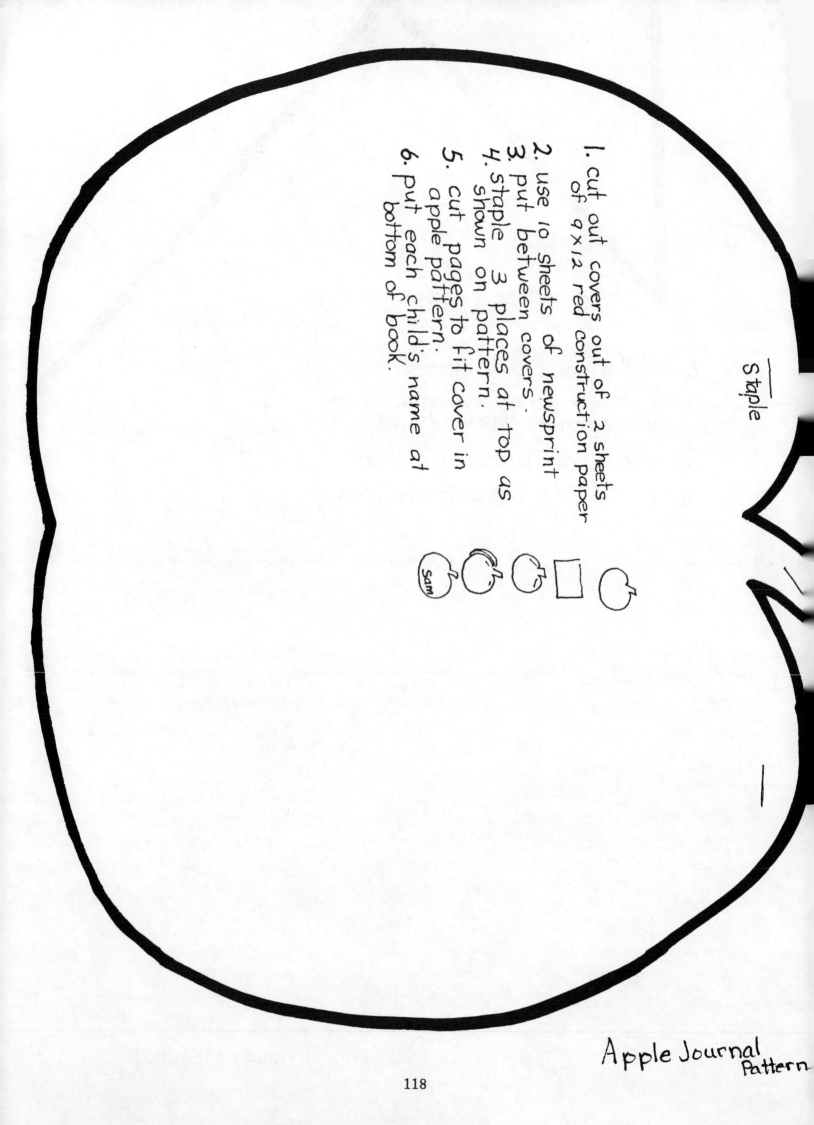

Staple

1. cut out covers out of 2 sheets of 9×12 red construction paper
2. use 10 sheets of newsprint
3. put between covers.
4. staple 3 places at top as shown on pattern.
5. cut pages to fit cover in apple pattern.
6. put each child's name at bottom of book.

Sam

Apple Journal
Pattern

INDEX

Apple Journal, pattern, 118
Apple Tree, fingerplay, 50
Applesauce, 48

Baked Egg Recipe, 21
Baker Clothing, pattern, 108, 109, 110
Balloon, A, fingerplay, 84
Basic Clothing Pattern Number 1, 93
Basic Clothing Pattern Number 2, 91, 92
Berenstain Bears Visit The Dentist, The, 34
Black, color, 51
Blue, color, 59
Body Parts, game, 38
Book, A, fingerplay, 42
Boy Doll, pattern, 90
Brave Police Officers, fingerplay, 62
Breakfast, fingerplay, 20
Brown, color, 43
Brush Your Teeth, fingerplay, 34
Butter, recipe, 64

Carrot and Potato Relay, game, 70
Chocolate Cake Cookies, 44
Coat and Hat, pattern, 95
Colors, see specific color
Cookies, Chocolate Cake, 44
Cow puzzle, 65
Curious George Goes To The Hospital, 57

Dentist, Outfit to go to, pattern,
   103, 104
Doctor and Nurse Clothing, pattern,
   111, 112, 113, 115
Doughnut Hole, fingerplay, 46

Farmer Clothing, pattern, 115, 116
Five Little Jack-O'-Lanterns,
   fingerplay, 80
Fire Fighter Clothing, pattern, 105, 106
Fishes, fingerplay, 28

Games, see titles
Gingerbread Boy, The, story, 3-5
Gingerbread Girls and Boys, 46
Girl Doll, pattern, 89
Going To Bed, fingerplay, 16
Grandma's, fingerplay, 16
Green, color, 47

Happy Me, fingerplay, 50
Happy Tooth-Sad Tooth, game, 33
House Journal Pattern, 117
How Many Teeth?, 34

I Can Be A Doctor, 57
I Can Be A Fire Fighter, 37

I'm a Little Teapot, fingerplay, 24
Imagine, fingerplay, 9

Jack Pumpkin Face, fingerplay, 79
Jeans Clothing, pattern, 107
Jimmy's House, fingerplay, 75

Little Cow, fingerplay, 66
Little Turtle, The, fingerplay, 27

Mr. Bump, 50
Mr. Carrot, fingerplay, 71
My Hair, fingerplay, 53

Night Clothing, pattern, 96, 97
Night Time, fingerplay, 17

Old MacDonald Had A Farm, song, 65
On The Bus, fingerplay, 12
One Little Child, fingerplay, 8
Orange, color, 77

Party Clothing, pattern, 100, 101
Pat-a-Cake, fingerplay, 45
Patterns, see titles
Police Officer!, game, 61
Police Officer Clothing, pattern, 106, 114
Puff, Puff, fingerplay, 84
Purple, color, 82
Puzzle, cow, 65

Recipes, see titles
Red, color, 35

Say Ah, film, 56
School Clothing, pattern, 98, 99
Silly Question, game, 81
Sleep, book, 15
Sleep Is For Everyone, book, 15
Stone Soup, 69
Swim Suits, pattern, 102

Ten Fingers And Ten Toes And Me,
   fingerplay, 29
Ten Fire Fighters, fingerplay, 37
Ten Little Fingers, fingerplay, 58
The Terrible Thing That Happened At
   Our House, 74
This Is Me, fingerplay, 8
Two Little Houses, fingerplay, 74
Two Little Men, fingerplay, 75

White, color, 31
Would You Shake?, fingerplay, 80

Yellow, color, 10